Agile Outsourcing

Using the CRAFTS Method to Capture Customer Value in
Outsourced Software Development

Joseph Pearce

Contents

Introduction

In an era where the pace of change is relentless and customer expectations are ever-evolving, Agile Outsourcing emerges as a beacon for organizations seeking to capture the elusive essence of customer value through software development. This paradigm isn't just a methodology; it's a revolution that harnesses the collective ingenuity of global talent pools to deliver outstanding digital experiences.

Agile Outsourcing is the synthesis of agility and global collaboration, a dynamic framework designed to propel businesses forward. It stands at the intersection of innovation and practicality, empowering teams to transcend geographical boundaries and cultural divides to create software that resonates with users on a profound level.

The ethos of Agile Outsourcing is built upon the pillars of the CRAFTS framework, which distills the essence of agile methodologies into a potent, customer-centric approach. It represents a strategic melding of 'Code delivery capability' with a 'Responsive Agile culture', underpinned by the adoption of scalable Agile processes that ensure seamless integration across diverse teams and landscapes.

At its core, Agile Outsourcing champions 'Fully integrated Team Ownership', encouraging a model where teams are not just executors of tasks but the custodians of the product vision. It nurtures a culture of 'Tireless Continuous Improvement', where the quest for perfection is a continuous journey, and 'Synchronized work' ensures that the sun never sets on the creative process, with teams around the world working in concert to bring innovations to life.

This introduction sets the stage for a transformative journey into the world of Agile Outsourcing, where the focus is not just on building software but on sculpting experiences that delight, engage, and retain customers. It's about leveraging the diversity of global teams to spark creativity and drive innovation, ensuring that every release is a step towards achieving unparalleled customer satisfaction.

As we delve into the realms of Agile Outsourcing, we invite you to embrace this journey with an open mind and a bold heart. It's a journey that promises to redefine the boundaries of software development and establish a new benchmark for capturing customer value in the digital age.

Who Should Read This?

This book is an essential read for managers, directors, and vice presidents of engineering and product who are navigating the complex terrain of outsourcing. It speaks directly to those who have never ventured into outsourcing, offering guidance to steer clear of common pitfalls and lay a strong foundation for successful outsourcing ventures.

For those who have experienced failures in outsourcing for various reasons, this book serves as a critical tool for understanding and rectifying past mistakes. It addresses common frustrations, such as the exhausting cycle of late-night calls and emergency meetings that disrupt work-life balance and the inefficiency of managing teams across time zones.

A significant challenge often encountered in outsourcing is the compromise on quality. If you've been frustrated by the subpar output of outsourced teams, which negates the advantage of lower costs, this book provides strategies to ensure quality and efficiency. It delves into the nuances of ensuring what is delivered aligns with customer needs and meets the high standards your product requires.

Miscommunication and misunderstandings are frequent in outsourced projects, leading to products that deviate from the original vision of the product teams. This book offers insights into bridging these communication gaps and aligning outsourced teams with your company's vision and goals.

High turnover in outsourced teams is another critical issue addressed in this book. It provides an analysis of the causes of this turnover and strategies to mitigate it, backed by relevant statistics. For instance, a study by Deloitte found that turnover rates in outsourcing centers can be as high as 40-50%, significantly impacting project continuity and knowledge retention.

Moreover, this book is crucial for those dealing with the internal dynamics and apprehensions surrounding outsourcing. If your internal teams feel threatened by the idea of outsourcing, concerned about job security or loss of influence, this book offers ways to navigate these changes and foster an environment of collaboration rather than competition.

This book is specifically crafted for teams engaged in software product development, encompassing a broad spectrum of applications from SaaS and mobile apps to mainframe code. The principles and methodologies discussed herein are universally applicable, offering valuable insights regardless of the nature or platform of the software being developed.

The core focus of this book is to apply agile principles to software product development. Agile methodologies, known for their flexibility and adaptability, are particularly effective in managing the dynamic and often unpredictable nature of software development. By adopting these agile practices, teams can enhance their productivity, responsiveness, and overall project management effectiveness.

While some of the principles outlined in this book may find relevance in IT service management, such as hosting email services, managing marketing websites, or other ticket-driven tasks, the primary focus remains on product development. IT service work, although crucial, often operates on different dynamics and may require a more tailored approach.

It is acknowledged that agile methodologies can also be applied to IT service work, offering potential improvements in efficiency and responsiveness. However, this book does not delve into those areas. The nature of IT service work, often characterized by its ticket-driven and reactive approach, differs significantly from the proactive and iterative nature of product development.

Finally, for organizations where outsourced teams feel marginalized, this book provides insights into creating an inclusive culture that values and integrates the contributions of all teams, regardless of their location.

In essence, this book is not just a guide to outsourcing; it's a roadmap for building a cohesive, efficient, and successful global team. Whether you are at the brink of initiating outsourcing or looking to refine your existing outsourcing strategies, the insights and strategies provided here are indispensable.

Onshoring is Offshoring

This book presents an Agile Outsourcing framework that transcends geographical boundaries, whether you are outsourcing to India, Eastern Europe, South America, or within the United States, such as Alabama. The core challenges of offshoring remain largely consistent across different regions, making the strategies and solutions offered in this book universally applicable.

Offshoring, at its core, involves dealing with an external organization. This external partnership often leads to a disconnection in power structures and processes, regardless of the location. The framework provided in this book addresses these challenges by offering agile methodologies and practices that foster better integration between the home base and offshore teams.

One of the central themes of this book is the management of disconnected power structures. Often, the parent company and the offshore team operate under different leadership and management styles, which can lead to a misalignment in goals and expectations. Our Agile Outsourcing framework provides tools and techniques to create a cohesive management approach that aligns both entities towards common objectives.

Another critical aspect that this book tackles is the issue of disconnected processes. Offshoring often results in fragmented workflows and communication barriers. The framework laid out in these pages offers robust strategies to streamline processes and enhance communication, ensuring that everyone is on the same page, regardless of their physical location.

It's important to note that while offshoring involves working with highly skilled, educated, and often well-compensated workers, cultural and regional nuances do exist. However, the problems arising from these nuances are not insurmountable. This book acknowledges these regional differences and provides insights into adapting the Agile Outsourcing framework to accommodate and leverage these unique regional traits.

The Agile Outsourcing framework discussed here is designed to be adaptable and flexible. It can be tailored to fit the specific needs and challenges of various regions while maintaining the core principles that make it effective. Whether you are dealing with time zone differences, cultural barriers, or varying business practices, the strategies in this book are crafted to be universally relevant and applicable.

In summary, this book is not just a guide to offshoring in a specific region. It's a comprehensive manual that addresses the universal challenges of outsourcing with a flexible, agile framework. It provides actionable insights and strategies that are effective in any outsourcing scenario, ensuring that your outsourcing efforts are successful, no matter where your partner is located.

The Agile Off-shoring Mindset

In the realm of outsourcing, the importance of processes and tools is undeniable. However, the heart of this book lies in advocating for an Agile philosophy, which transcends mere practicalities. Agile is more than a methodology; it is a mindset, an ethos that must permeate every aspect of project management and team dynamics. This section delves into the crucial role of the right management mindset and the conditioning necessary for teams to thrive in an outsourcing environment.

At the forefront of this Agile mindset is the cultivation of a respectful, team-aligning approach. The success of outsourcing hinges not just on technical prowess or process efficiency but on the ability to foster a collaborative and inclusive culture. This book emphasizes the significance of avoiding an 'us versus them' mentality, which can easily creep into outsourced project dynamics. Such a divisive outlook breeds a toxic environment, hampering the collective efforts of the team.

Equally detrimental is the emergence of a scapegoat culture, where blame is passed around rather than solutions being sought collaboratively. This book advocates for a culture where responsibility is shared, and challenges are addressed collectively. As a manager, it becomes imperative to extend your responsibility beyond mere oversight. It involves taking ownership of not just the engineers under your direct supervision but of the entire product and every individual contributing to it, regardless of their geographical location.

Humility plays a pivotal role in this Agile philosophy. Setting aside personal pride and embracing humility is not a sign of weakness; rather, it is a strength that fosters learning, growth, and collaboration. This book encourages managers and team leaders to adopt a humble approach, acknowledging that outsourcing is a learning journey for everyone involved. It is about listening, being open to new ideas, and admitting that there is always room for improvement.

This Agile philosophy is not about relinquishing control but about redefining it. It's about leading with empathy, understanding, and respect. It involves acknowledging the diverse perspectives and strengths that each team member, whether local or offshore, brings to the table. By doing so, you pave the way for a more harmonious, productive, and ultimately successful outsourcing endeavor.

In essence, the Agile philosophy advocated in this book is about creating a respectful, collaborative, and humble work environment. It's about understanding that the right mindset is as crucial as the right tools and processes. With this philosophy at the core, outsourcing can transform from a challenging endeavor into an enriching, rewarding experience that drives the success of the entire organization.

Focus on Software

This book is dedicated exclusively to the world of software outsourcing, encompassing the vast and varied landscape of software development. It delves into the intricacies of outsourcing in diverse software domains, whether it be enterprise solutions, consumer applications, mobile technologies, or server-based platforms. The focus is tightly centered on the unique challenges and opportunities that these areas present when navigating the outsourcing terrain.

Software development, with its own set of nuances and complexities, requires a specialized approach, especially in an outsourcing context. This book aims to provide insights and strategies that are particularly relevant and effective for software projects. Whether you are developing a sophisticated enterprise system, a consumer-facing mobile app, or robust server-side solutions, the principles and practices outlined here are tailored to guide you through the specific demands of these software categories.

It's important to acknowledge that while the Agile philosophy and many of the management strategies discussed in this book may have broader applications, the focus remains steadfastly on software. This is primarily due to the author's expertise and depth of experience in the software outsourcing sector. The realm of outsourcing extends beyond software to areas such as call centers and business process outsourcing (BPO). However, these domains have their own unique set of dynamics, challenges, and best practices, which are outside the scope of this book.

Outsourcing in software development involves a multitude of factors – from handling technical complexities, managing software project lifecycles, ensuring quality in code development, to aligning product outcomes with client expectations. This book provides a comprehensive exploration of these aspects, offering readers a clear and focused guide on achieving success in software outsourcing.

In summary, this book is a dedicated resource for professionals involved in software outsourcing. It brings to the forefront the critical elements that influence the success of outsourcing in the software industry, providing valuable insights and practical strategies that are specifically suited to this field. While the overarching principles of effective outsourcing management might be universally applicable, the specific focus here remains firmly on the software sector.

Why I Am Qualified to Write This Book

My journey through the landscape of software development outsourcing is etched with two decades of rich, hands-on experience. This section offers a glimpse into my professional journey and the credentials that position me as a trusted guide in the world of outsourcing, particularly in software development.

Over these years, I have been at the helm of building and scaling software development teams, starting from the ground up. My experience spans creating initial team structures to expanding them across diverse product portfolios. This journey has not only been about expansion but also about nurturing a culture of excellence. I pride myself on my track record of producing high-quality software, a testament to my commitment to engineering precision and innovative thinking.

However, the path has not always been smooth. I have encountered my fair share of challenges – failed projects, middle-of-the-night crisis calls, and the arduous task of addressing quality issues. These experiences, though tough, were invaluable learning opportunities. They equipped me with an acute understanding of the pitfalls in outsourcing and how to navigate them successfully. My insights are not just theoretical but are born from real-world experiences of what works and what doesn't in the complex realm of software outsourcing.

At Coalfire Systems, Inc., where I served as Vice President of Technology and Engineering, I led the growth of a global technology team, scaling it to hundreds of professionals across multiple continents. My leadership was instrumental in the strategic acquisition and integration of two cybersecurity software firms, enhancing productivity and reducing customer issues significantly. My tenure saw the successful transition to cloud-native computing and the implementation of advanced DevOps practices, underscoring my technical acumen and forward-thinking approach.

My technical skills are underpinned by a strong educational foundation, with an Executive MBA from Duke University's Fuqua School of Business and a Bachelor of Science in Computer Engineering from the Florida Institute of Technology. These academic pursuits, combined with my professional experience, have honed my abilities in strategic vision, team building, and aligning engineering strategies with business objectives.

Recognition of my work has come not only from the teams I have led but also from industry peers and leaders. I have been ranked in the top 5% of engineering organizations worldwide and have been lauded as an indispensable employee during acquisition processes. These accolades speak to my ability to inspire innovation and drive technological advancement.

In summary, my journey through the realms of software development and outsourcing is marked by a blend of technical mastery, strategic leadership, and a deep understanding of the challenges and opportunities in outsourcing. This book is a culmination of these experiences and learnings, crafted to guide you through the complexities of outsourcing in software development with a hands-on, experienced approach.

Introduction

For many years, I had a group chat with my friends from high school. They are all a very smart, well educated, group of gentlemen that have taken very different life paths.

After high school Kevin studied law and became a lawyer. He went on to clerk at the New Mexico Supreme Court and he spent years focusing on social justice issues. Today, he develops software.

Another friend, Rob, took the chemistry route and obtained his PhD in Chemistry. After university he went on to develop atomic layer deposition products. Today, he works for Amazon in their machine learning division.

Dan had a passion for hospitality. His talents took him to owning an upscale restaurant in the Financial District of San Francisco and a brew-pub in Atlanta. I have been to both restaurants and they were excellent. Today he develops retail software.

The final friend in this group, Alex, went the software route out of college, like I did, and remains in the industry working on high-end enterprise and government systems.

The reason I bring these gentlemen up is because of the massive brain gain that occurs in the software industry. Smart people, from all industries, are being coaxed into software development. The Bureau of Labor and Statistics estimates that there are just shy of 2 million people working in software development and quality assurance, and that the job growth will continue at 22% over a 10 year period. ("Software Developers, Quality Assurance Analysts, and Testers : Occupational Outlook Handbook : US Bureau of Labor Statistics")

The statistics match up with the reality on the ground.

Web 2.0 has gone mainstream. Companies that were using desktop software before have nearly all converted to using interactive web software. Companies that were never impacted by technology in the past, now require it to remain competitive or have already been replaced by digital business models.

While Web 2.0 will have an impact for the coming decade, innovative companies are already preparing for the next wave of technological disruptors. The foundational technology behind Web 3.0 is now coming together allowing fully distributed enterprises to exist. By the end of the decade, the quantum revolution will require a complete rethink of communication, security, and data processing among countless other impacts we are only starting to be able to predict.

All of this innovation means that we are going to need millions of additional software developers. Very few companies will be able to fulfill their software strategies with strictly domestic staff, and will be forced to turn to the global outsourced software market to meet their sourcing demands.

Why Companies Outsource

I ordered a pizza on Dominos.com the other day. I was impressed at how they have taken a very traditional business and digitally transformed it into a software-led service. From the moment I entered my order I was able to use the Pizza Tracker to know when my pizza was in the oven, when it was being boxed, and when it left for delivery. They even calculated within 1 minute when that pizza would be at my door. This begs the question as to whether Dominos has more software developers employed or more chefs in their test kitchens innovating on their pizza recipes. Either way, Dominos has had to staff up dozens of software developers in the previous years.

As they sourced their engineers, they had to make the same choices many of us software development managers have to make on a regular basis. Do we try to recruit locally or at least domestically, or do we outsource?

In an ideal world, we could find the talented engineers we need in our local market, all work in the same office, and hold all of our agile ceremonies together in a large conference room over planning pizza, but we rarely have this luxury. In general, there are three reasons why we would look to hire outsourced software developers, testers, or other tangential fields:

Costs

In the early days of software outsourcing, the primary driver was costs. It was possible to hire a software development team out of India for a blended rate of $17/hour when local engineers would cost 4 times this rate. While everybody hated the 12 or so hour time difference, the economics were simply too strong.

In the early days of my career at a large health insurance company, this was the business driver that led us to recruiting the majority of our team from overseas.

Recruiting

The big FAANGs (Facebook, Apple, Amazon, Netflix, and Google) of the world have top engineering talent knocking on their door by the minute, and yet they still must look at outsourcing to meet their staffing needs. For the other 99% of the industry, it is even more difficult to recruit and retain the software development talent needed to accomplish our business needs.

Later in my career, this was the problem I ran into. I was at a small Seattle based company that was primarily known for its services rather than its products. For months we tried to recruit against Microsoft and Facebook, but we found that we were scraping the bottom of the barrel for talent. When we began to look overseas, we found that in smaller markets like South America our projects were desirable and exciting enough to recruit truly top notch talent.

Increased Time to Market

The third most common reason for outsourcing is for rather mature groups that want to get their products to market faster or provide around the clock operational support. Generally, these companies have very mature software development practices and have developed a smooth hand-off process between their domestic staff and their staff located on the other side of the world. I will speak about synchronized methodologies later in this book.

Other Benefits to Outsourcing

Going with an outsourced model comes with other advantages on top of the primary drivers as well. This includes:

Reduced Back Office Overhead

Outsourcing software development extends beyond the mere delegation of tasks; it represents a strategic shift in reducing the back-office overhead associated with maintaining an in-house staff. This chapter delves into the nuances of how outsourcing impacts not only the cost structures of a company but also enhances its focus and operational efficiency.

When a company decides to outsource its software development, it effectively offloads a significant portion of its administrative responsibilities. This includes the management of payroll, human resources, partial IT support, and benefits management associated with the staff. The implications of this are profound, as it leads to a more streamlined back-office operation, freeing up valuable resources and time. This shift allows companies to redirect their focus from internal administrative tasks to more critical business activities, including customer engagement and core business processes.

However, this transition to outsourcing is accompanied by certain trade-offs, particularly in terms of control over staff management. For example, when you outsource, the ability to make decisions about salary adjustments or promotions is no longer in your hands but is governed by the outsourcing provider's policies. This lack of direct control can sometimes lead to discrepancies in role mapping and compensation, particularly when there's a mismatch between the outsourcing provider's assessment and your own standards. To navigate this, it's crucial to establish open and honest communication with your provider. Engaging in negotiations over individual rates or role assignments and allowing for trial periods to assess performance are effective strategies to ensure alignment.

Furthermore, outsourcing necessitates a keen understanding and negotiation of offboarding terms. While outsourcing firms generally strive to maintain client satisfaction and are often flexible in personnel reassignment, being aware of any contractual implications is crucial for smooth transitions. This is especially important in scenarios where staff reassignment is required.

An often-overlooked aspect of outsourcing is the limitations it places on your internal HR processes. Contractors, who may be core to your company's success, do not partake in your internal review processes, bonus schemes, or company events. This is particularly true when these contractors are based thousands of miles away, which can create a sense of disconnect from your company culture.

In summary, while outsourcing software development offers substantial benefits in terms of reducing overhead and sharpening business focus, it also demands a strategic approach in managing the outsourced team. Companies embarking on this path need to balance the advantages of outsourcing with effective management of the associated challenges. This involves clear communication, smart contract negotiations, and an adaptable approach to managing outsourced relationships. By embracing these strategies, businesses can integrate outsourcing into their operational model successfully, leveraging its benefits while maintaining high standards of project execution and team dynamics.

More Mature Processes

In your quest to refine your Agile Outsourcing processes, a pivotal strategy is to collaborate with a well-established vendor experienced in working across diverse geographies. Such vendors, though rare, bring a depth of knowledge and expertise in project management and technology operations, essential for owning and successfully executing comprehensive projects.

Consider the case of a company venturing into the gaming platform industry, helmed by individuals whose expertise lay in finance, particularly student loans, rather than software development. Their initial approach to software requirements was scattered, driven more by ideas than a clear roadmap for implementation. This scenario is not uncommon; businesses often find themselves adept in their core area but novice in transforming conceptual ideas into tangible software products.

This organization, however, made a strategic decision to outsource to a firm with a mature product development process that adhered to agile principles. The result was a transformational experience. The outsourcing partner's agility and experience in managing a constantly evolving stream of ideas were crucial. They were able to release incremental updates and features on a weekly basis, adapting swiftly to the client's changing needs. In this context, outsourcing became not just a necessity but a catalyst for the company's growth and betterment.

The experience of working with outsourcing partners can also be a learning journey. These partners are exposed to a wide array of companies, gaining a global perspective, especially at the management level where insights across different products are accumulated. A proficient outsourcing partner not only delivers on specific projects but also fosters communities for shared learning, offering exposure to best-in-industry practices observed across various clients.

For any organization, no matter how mature its processes may seem, there is always room for improvement. This is a core tenet of agile methodology—continuous improvement. By actively listening to and learning from your outsourcing partners, you can gain valuable insights into different ways of working, novel approaches to problem-solving, and innovative practices. This can lead to significant enhancements in your own processes and methodologies.

In summary, leveraging the experience and maturity of an outsourced firm can greatly benefit your Agile Outsourcing endeavors. It's not just about delegating tasks but about embracing the wealth of knowledge and best practices these firms bring. The key lies in choosing the right partner—one that not only claims expertise but demonstrates it through successful cross-geographical projects and a robust, agile approach. By doing so, you not only ensure the successful execution of your projects but also open doors to continuous learning and process improvement, which are essential in the ever-evolving landscape of software development.

Leveraging Networks of Expertise in Outsourced Software Development

When engaging with an outsourcing vendor for software development, you're not just hiring a team; you're tapping into a network of specialized expertise. Whether your outsourcing partner is smaller or larger than your company, their specialization in software development and the pride they take in their expertise are critical assets. This expertise is often what sets them apart in a competitive market where they vie not just on price but on knowledge and skill as well.

In the journey of software development, encountering technical hurdles is inevitable. Sometimes, these challenges can be so complex that your in-house team might find themselves at a standstill, unable to devise a solution. In such scenarios, you generally have a couple of options.

The first option is to bring in an external specialized expert. While this approach can bring in the needed expertise, it often comes with its set of challenges - it's expensive, time-consuming, and necessitates additional contracts and onboarding processes.

The second, often more efficient option is to leverage the internal network of your outsourcing team. A notable advantage of working with an outsourcing firm is their ecosystem of specialized communities. These communities are typically composed of professionals with deep expertise in specific technologies like Angular, AWS scalability,

Snowflake, MongoDB, and more. These experts frequently collaborate, sharing knowledge and staying abreast of the latest developments in their fields.

When faced with a particularly daunting technical challenge, your outsourced team can tap into this internal network. They can consult with their colleagues who specialize in the relevant technology, drawing on their collective knowledge to find a solution. This approach can often lead to solving complex problems more efficiently than bringing in external consultants.

It's important to foster a spirit of reciprocity in this ecosystem. There may be times when your team lends their expertise to assist other teams within the outsourcing firm. While it might seem like a diversion of resources initially, this collaborative environment typically benefits all parties involved. The knowledge and solutions gained from such interactions often flow back to your projects, enriching your team's capabilities and contributing to the overall success of your endeavors.

In conclusion, the value of an outsourcing firm extends beyond the immediate team working on your project. It includes access to a broader network of expertise that can prove invaluable, especially when facing complex technical challenges. By understanding and appreciating this interconnected network of knowledge, you can effectively navigate the intricacies of software development, turning potential roadblocks into opportunities for innovation and growth. Remember, in the realm of outsourced software development, the strength lies not just in individual expertise but in the collective wisdom of a community.

Dynamically Scalable Teams in Outsourcing

One of the most significant advantages of outsourcing in software development is the ability to dynamically scale teams according to the evolving needs of your project. This flexibility is a stark contrast to the more static nature of traditional employment, where the assumption is an ongoing, long-term relationship.

In most outsourced contracts, the terms often include termination clauses that allow for the scaling down of resources with relatively short notice, typically around 30 days. This feature is particularly advantageous when there's a need to pivot your strategy or when a specific initiative requires downsizing. It provides the flexibility to reduce spending and reallocate resources more efficiently in response to changing business needs.

However, it's important to approach this flexibility judiciously. Over-utilizing the ability to downsize can undermine the investment in your team's development and potentially disrupt the continuity and morale of the team. While it's a valuable tool for adapting to strategic shifts, it should be used thoughtfully to maintain a stable and committed team environment.

Conversely, outsourcing offers a remarkable ability to scale up quickly. For instance, there have been scenarios where a sudden need arose to add a significant number of people, say 30, to a team in a short period. By leveraging both the company's internal recruiting resources and the outsourced vendor's network, or even multiple vendors, you effectively double or triple the capacity to recruit new talent quickly. However, it's crucial to ensure that your team's culture and processes can accommodate and adapt to this rapid expansion. The integration of new members must be managed carefully to maintain the team's cohesion and effectiveness.

Whether scaling up or down, it's vital to have robust onboarding and offboarding practices in place. This ensures that all changes are in compliance with your company's internal policies and legal requirements. Proper onboarding is essential for quickly integrating new members and aligning them with your team's culture and processes. Similarly, effective offboarding ensures that transitions out of the team are handled professionally and securely, safeguarding any sensitive information and maintaining compliance.

In summary, the dynamic scalability of teams is a significant advantage in outsourcing software development. It allows for a responsive approach to changing project requirements and strategic pivots. However, this flexibility should be balanced with a commitment to team stability and compliance with internal policies. Proper management of team dynamics, whether scaling up or down, is essential for maintaining the effectiveness and integrity of your software development efforts.

Geographic Diversification

Geographic diversification represents a strategic imperative for multinational corporations aiming to expand their reach and bolster resilience. By distributing resources across various regions, companies can tap into the dual benefits of cost reduction and the exploitation of favorable trade agreements and government policies. This strategy is not chosen at random; companies meticulously weigh factors such as regional competitiveness, cultural alignment, political climate, and currency stability to make informed decisions.

In an increasingly interconnected world, geographic diversification goes beyond mere cost savings. It serves as a hedge against regional instabilities and economic downturns. By establishing a presence in multiple geographies, companies are not only able to mitigate risks associated with any single market but are also well-positioned to capture growth opportunities across the globe. For instance, an economic crisis in one region may be counterbalanced by robust performance in another, ensuring overall stability and continued growth for the business.

Furthermore, geographic diversification aligns with broader growth strategies that include tapping into emerging markets, accessing new talent pools, and fostering innovation through diverse cultural perspectives. It enables companies to become global players, ready to take advantage of shifting market dynamics and consumer trends, and to respond agilely to changes in the global economic landscape. In essence, geographic diversification is not just a defensive strategy; it is a proactive approach to secure a competitive edge, drive growth, and build a sustainable, future-proof business.

Embracing Digital Transformation through Outsourced Firms

In an era where technology-driven business models are reshaping industries, the ability to adapt and evolve has become critical for companies to stay competitive. From traditional taxi services grappling with the rise of Uber to hotels contending with Airbnb, the impact of technological innovation is undeniable. Even services like notarization, which traditionally required in-person interactions, have moved online, offering convenience through digital platforms.

For many established companies, especially those steeped in traditional business models, undergoing a digital transformation can be daunting. These organizations often lack the inherent DNA for a digital makeover, operating in a world where modern technological advances seem alien. In such scenarios, outsourced firms specializing in digital transformation can be invaluable. They offer an injection of modernity, enabling businesses to integrate new technologies and processes without disrupting their core operations.

However, the success of this transformation hinges on a company's willingness to embrace change. Merely implementing new technologies or processes superficially, without letting them redefine the core business model, limits the potential benefits. It's not just about adopting digital solutions but about allowing these solutions to transform how the business operates fundamentally.

For instance, a retail business moving its inventory to an online platform gains more than just an additional sales channel. It opens up opportunities for data analytics, personalized marketing, and customer engagement strategies that were previously unattainable. Similarly, a manufacturing company adopting IoT and AI can optimize production processes, reduce waste, and enhance product quality in ways that traditional methods couldn't achieve.

Resistance to change, especially in favor of old-world models, can stifle growth and innovation. Clinging to "golden geese" – the traditional revenue streams or business practices – might provide short-term comfort but can lead to long-term stagnation. The real value of partnering with outsourced technology firms lies in their ability to challenge the status quo, bringing fresh perspectives and expertise that can unlock new avenues for growth and efficiency.

In conclusion, leveraging outsourced firms to transform your business model is not just a strategy for IT implementation; it's a pathway to reimagine and revitalize your business in the digital age. It requires an openness to change, a willingness to let go of outdated practices, and a vision to see beyond the immediate horizon. By doing so, companies can not only keep pace with their competition but can set the stage to lead and define the future of their industries.

Method to Hire in Other Countries

In the dynamic world of global business, companies often encounter unique scenarios that demand innovative solutions. One such edge case involves hiring employees in foreign countries where the organization lacks local operational knowledge. This section explores how outsourcing can be a strategic tool for such situations, drawing from a real-life example of hiring in Uruguay.

When a company expands or acquires new business interests in a country where it has no prior presence, the challenges are multifaceted. This was precisely the case when there was a need to onboard about 10 new employees in Uruguay following an acquisition. The primary hurdles included unfamiliarity with local employment laws, cultural nuances, and administrative processes, including payroll management. In such situations, the limitations of an otherwise robust HR department become evident, especially when it's unacquainted with the legal and socio-economic landscape of the new region.

To navigate this challenge, turning to an outsourced partner proved to be a strategic and effective solution. Outsourcing firms specializing in international employment can offer invaluable support in such scenarios. These firms are equipped with the necessary expertise in local employment laws, payroll processing, and HR management specific to the region.

1. Local Expertise: Outsourcing partners bring onboard their extensive knowledge of local labor laws, tax regulations, and employment practices. This expertise is crucial for ensuring compliance and avoiding legal pitfalls.
2. Streamlined Payroll and Administration: Handling payroll in a foreign country can be complex due to different tax systems, benefit schemes, and compliance requirements. Outsourcing firms can manage these aspects efficiently, ensuring that employees are paid correctly and on time.
3. Rapid Onboarding: The process of setting up operations in a new country, including the establishment of a local HR department, can be time-consuming and resource-intensive. Outsourcing accelerates this process, allowing for quick integration of new employees.
4. Cost-Effectiveness: Setting up a full-fledged HR operation in a new country for a relatively small team may not be cost-effective. Outsourcing offers a more economical solution without the long-term commitment of establishing a local entity.
5. 5. Risk Mitigation: By leveraging the expertise of a local outsourcing partner, companies can significantly reduce the risks associated with non-compliance and cultural misunderstandings.

In the specific case of Uruguay, utilizing an outsourced HR service enabled the seamless integration of the new employees into the company. This approach provided a practical solution to bridge the gap between the company's existing HR capabilities and the requirements of operating in a new jurisdiction. It ensured that the new team members were onboarded efficiently, with all legal and administrative aspects handled adeptly by the outsourcing partner.

This example underscores the versatility of outsourcing as a strategic tool, not just for typical business processes but also for addressing specific, uncommon challenges like hiring in a new country. By tapping into the specialized services of outsourced HR and payroll providers, companies can expand their global footprint more confidently, ensuring that they remain focused on their core business activities while the intricacies of local employment are managed expertly.

Business Continuity

For modern enterprises, the choice to outsource is increasingly driven by the need for business continuity. As companies grapple with the complexities of global operations amid a landscape fraught with uncertainties, the strategic distribution of resources through outsourcing has become vital. This process, often part of a larger geographic diversification strategy, allows companies to not only reduce costs but also to capitalize on favorable regional trade policies and government incentives.

The decision-making process for outsourcing is thorough and deliberate, where companies evaluate a myriad of factors including regional market competitiveness, cultural compatibility, political stability, and the robustness of local currencies. Such a multifaceted approach ensures that the selected outsourcing destinations align with the company's broader strategic objectives.

The benefits of geographic diversification are manifold, extending far beyond cost-effectiveness. It acts as a safeguard against the volatility of regional economies, ensuring that a downturn in one area can be offset by stability or growth in another. This strategic positioning across diverse markets enables companies to withstand local shocks and maintain operational fluidity, which is crucial for sustaining business momentum.

Geographic diversification also aligns with the pursuit of growth, enabling companies to penetrate emerging markets, harness fresh talent, and imbibe varied cultural insights, thereby spurring innovation. This global footprint empowers companies to be at the forefront of market trends and consumer behaviors, allowing for swift adaptation to the ever-evolving economic environment.

Thus, geographic diversification through outsourcing is more than a mere tactical move; it is an integral component of a proactive business strategy. It equips companies with the agility to navigate the complexities of the global economy, ensuring a competitive advantage, fostering sustainable growth, and securing the longevity of the business in an unpredictable world.

Learn About Your Customers Through Your Team

Expanding into new markets requires not just an understanding of the business landscape but also a deep insight into local customer preferences and behaviors. This is where your outsourced team can be an invaluable asset, especially when they are based in the target market. For instance, if you're a bicycle sharing company eyeing expansion into Poland, having a Polish software development team can provide you with a wealth of local knowledge that is essential for your product's success.

An outsourced team in Poland can offer more than just technical expertise; they bring a nuanced understanding of the local culture, consumer behavior, and market dynamics. This local knowledge is crucial in tailoring your services to meet the unique needs and preferences of Polish customers. They can provide insights into local commuting patterns, popular routes, and preferences that might be different from your current markets.

When deploying new features tailored to the Polish market, your local outsourced team can serve as an invaluable sanity check. They can evaluate whether these features align with local expectations and cultural norms. For instance, they can advise on the most appealing incentives for Polish users to use your bicycle sharing service, or suggest features that address specific local challenges.

Expanding into a new country often comes with language barriers and cultural differences that can hinder effective communication and market understanding. Your Polish team can bridge these gaps, ensuring that your marketing messages resonate with the local audience and that your product interface is intuitive and culturally relevant. They can also assist in translating and localizing your app or website, making it more accessible and user-friendly for Polish customers.

Your outsourced team can also play a key role in conducting localized market research and gathering feedback. They can help design and implement surveys, focus groups, or other research methods to gather authentic insights from Polish users. This feedback can be crucial in refining your product offering and ensuring it meets the specific needs of the local market.

Outsourced teams can act as brand ambassadors in their local community. Their first-hand experience with your product and deep understanding of your brand can help in spreading positive word-of-mouth and building trust among potential customers. This is particularly effective in markets where local endorsements and recommendations are highly valued.

Using your outsourced team to gain insights into your customers is not just practical but strategic. It allows you to tap into local expertise and knowledge, ensuring your expansion efforts are well-informed and culturally sensitive. By leveraging the unique perspective and skills of your Polish software development team, you can significantly increase your chances of success in the new market, making your venture into Poland not just a leap of faith but a calculated and informed step forward.

Navigating the Complexities of Software Outsourcing

Software development outsourcing, a strategy increasingly adopted by companies to harness global expertise and cost efficiency, comes with its share of complexities. The high failure rate in such endeavors, as reported by Dun & Bradstreet, where 20-25% of outsourcing relationships fail within two years, escalating to 50% within five years, underscores the need for a deeper understanding and strategic approach to address these multifaceted challenges. Companies that are new to outsourcing generally have the same few major, and real, concerns.

Navigating the Challenges of Technical Expertise and Expectations in Software Outsourcing

Software outsourcing, while offering numerous benefits, often encounters the significant challenge of aligning technical expertise with client expectations. This misalignment, stemming from varied understanding and objectives, can lead to project inefficiencies and unmet goals.

One of the primary issues faced in software outsourcing is the disparity between what clients expect and what is technically feasible or practical. Companies sometimes enter into outsourcing agreements with a limited grasp of the software development process. This lack of deep technical knowledge can lead to unrealistic expectations regarding the capabilities, timelines, and budgets of a project.

Clients might envision complex features or technological solutions without fully understanding the implications in terms of development time and resources. This gap in understanding often results in demands for unnecessary or overly costly features, leading to inflated budgets and extended timelines.

Inadequate technical insight can also lead to poor decisions in technology selection. Companies might opt for the latest or most hyped technologies without considering whether these are the best fit for their specific project needs. Such choices not only inflate project costs but also can lead to long-term maintenance challenges and compatibility issues.

Another critical aspect where expectations diverge from reality is in the estimation of project costs and timeframes. Without a clear understanding of the software development lifecycle, companies can underestimate the time and resources required for project completion. This often results in projects exceeding budgets and missing deadlines, leading to frustration and potential conflicts with outsourcing partners.

To mitigate these challenges, it is essential for companies to:

1. Enhance Communication: Establish clear, ongoing communication channels with the outsourcing team. Regular updates and discussions can help in aligning expectations with practical realities.
2. Educate and Inform: Companies should invest time in understanding the basics of software development processes. This knowledge can aid in setting more realistic expectations and making more informed decisions.
3. Seek Expert Consultation: Leveraging the expertise of technical consultants or in-house IT professionals can help in making informed decisions about technology selection and project scopes.
4. Realistic Planning: Embrace a pragmatic approach in project planning. Understand that good software development often requires flexibility, and adjustments may be needed as the project evolves.
5. 5. Collaborative Approach: Work in partnership with the outsourcing team, valuing their technical expertise and insights.

This collaborative approach can help in identifying potential issues early and finding effective solutions.

The gap between technical expertise and client expectations in software outsourcing presents a significant challenge but is not insurmountable. By fostering better communication, educating themselves about the development process, and taking a more collaborative approach, companies can effectively bridge this gap. This alignment is crucial for the successful completion of outsourced software projects, ensuring that the final product aligns with both technical realities and business objectives.

The Perils of Choosing the Cheapest Software Outsourcing Vendors

In the realm of software outsourcing, the allure of cost savings can often lead companies to opt for the cheapest available vendors. However, this approach can be fraught with hidden costs and unforeseen challenges, as highlighted in Deloitte's report, which reveals that while 59% of companies expect to save money through outsourcing, the reality can be quite different.

Choosing the lowest bidder in software development outsourcing might seem financially prudent initially, but it often masks several hidden costs that can accumulate over time, negating any initial savings. These costs manifest in various ways:

1. High Turnover Rates: Inexpensive outsourcing firms often have high employee turnover rates, sometimes as high as 30%. High turnover not only incurs additional costs in recruiting and training new team members but also leads to project delays and loss of accumulated knowledge and expertise.
2. Compromised Quality: Cheaper vendors might cut corners to keep costs low, resulting in software of inferior quality. This can lead to a proliferation of bugs and issues in the product,

necessitating further investment in fixes and improvements, thus driving up the total cost of ownership.

3. Impact on Customer Satisfaction: Subpar software directly impacts customer satisfaction and can adversely affect a company's reputation and customer loyalty. Poor user experience can lead to a decline in Net Promoter Scores (NPS), indicating lower customer loyalty and potential loss of future business.

In light of these factors, it's crucial for companies to shift their focus from merely considering the upfront costs to evaluating the overall value provided by an outsourcing partner. This involves considering:

- Expertise and Experience: Evaluate the technical expertise and industry experience of the vendor. More experienced vendors, though initially more expensive, can provide higher quality work, reducing the need for rework.

- Quality Assurance Practices: Assess the quality assurance measures the vendor has in place. Robust testing and QA processes can prevent costly errors and ensure a smoother, more reliable software development lifecycle.

- Communication and Project Management: Good communication and efficient project management are essential for successful project execution. Vendors who invest in these aspects are more likely to deliver projects on time and within budget.

- Long-term Partnership Potential: Consider the potential for a long-term partnership. A vendor who understands your business and is invested in your success can offer strategic benefits beyond mere cost savings.

The choice of a software outsourcing vendor should not be driven solely by cost considerations. While budget constraints are a reality for many companies, the cheapest option can often lead to increased total costs in the long run due to factors like high turnover, quality issues, and the impact on customer satisfaction. A more balanced approach that weighs cost against value, expertise, and long-term benefits is essential for achieving successful and sustainable outcomes in software outsourcing.

Navigating Communication Challenges in Outsourced Software Development

Effective communication is a cornerstone of successful software development outsourcing. However, companies often encounter significant communication barriers, particularly when teams are spread across different cultures and time zones. These challenges can lead to misaligned objectives, frequent changes in requirements, and unclear project goals, thereby hindering the overall success of the project.

In an ideal Agile product development environment, open and seamless communication between the product team and every member of the development team is crucial. This synergy minimizes bugs and ensures the most effective rollout of software value. However, language barriers can pose a significant obstacle. It's a common misconception that language differences will impede communication entirely. Surprisingly, English, being the global language of business, is widely spoken among professionals worldwide. This commonality can ease the communication process, especially with more experienced team members. For junior developers, who may not be as proficient in English, alternative communication strategies can be employed.

Cultural differences in work and communication styles can also impact the effectiveness of collaboration. Approaching these differences with humility and a willingness to learn is crucial. For instance, in regions like Colombia, the work culture tends to be more hierarchical, with less emphasis on collaborative management styles. This cultural trait can affect how teams interact and share feedback.

To build strong relationships and encourage open communication, it's essential to engage in team-building activities. Sharing meals or casual social gatherings can significantly improve rapport and understanding among team members. In situations where language barriers exist, asking team members to repeat or paraphrase what has been communicated can ensure mutual understanding. Moreover, written communication can be invaluable. Documenting discussions and decisions allows team members to revisit and comprehend information at their own pace, which is especially helpful for those who may feel apprehensive about language differences.

1. Encourage Regular Check-Ins: Establish regular check-ins and meetings to ensure everyone is on the same page. Video conferencing tools can help bridge the gap between different locations.
2. Utilize Collaboration Tools: Leverage project management and collaboration tools that facilitate clear task assignments and progress tracking. Tools like Jira, Trello, or Slack can be instrumental in maintaining clear and organized communication.
3. Invest in Cultural Training: Provide cultural training for your teams to foster an understanding of different work and communication styles. This investment can pay dividends in terms of team cohesion and productivity.
4. Emphasize Clarity and Conciseness: Encourage clear and concise communication. Avoid jargon and complex language, especially when working with teams for whom English is a second language.
5. Foster a Feedback Culture: Create an environment where feedback is encouraged and valued. This approach helps identify misunderstandings early and aligns the team towards common goals.

In conclusion, while communication challenges in outsourced software development are real, they are not insurmountable. By adopting a proactive approach that includes cultural sensitivity, clear and concise communication, and the use of collaborative tools, companies can effectively bridge the communication gap. This section sets the stage for a deeper dive into effective communication practices in Agile teams, which will be explored later in this book.

Developer Quality and Team Dynamics

The success of outsourced software development projects hinges significantly on the quality of the development team engaged. When companies opt for outsourcing, the focus often shifts towards cost-efficiency, sometimes at the expense of quality. This approach can lead to a cascade of issues that not only affect the immediate project but also have long-term implications on the overall business strategy.

Engaging low-quality developers, often lured by lower costs, can result in substandard code, leading to project delays and budget overruns. This choice often leads to 'technical debt', where quick and easy solutions are chosen over the right solutions, creating more problems down the line. Additionally, a mismatch between the team size and the scope of the project can lead to inefficiencies. A common outcome is 'scope creep' - a gradual expansion of the project beyond its original objectives, often causing significant shifts in timelines and budgets.

A successful outsourcing partnership is not just about technical skills; it also requires a deep alignment in terms of business vision, work ethics, and commitment to the project's success. This alignment is crucial for ensuring that the outsourced team not only understands the technical requirements but also grasps the broader business objectives and works in sync with the company's ethos.

Companies must be wary of the allure of the lowest bid. While initial cost savings might seem attractive, this can lead to increased expenditure in the long run. Poor workmanship and communication issues are common with lower-cost providers, often necessitating expensive reworks and causing project delays. The additional time spent on correcting these issues and the potential impact on the product's market launch can outweigh the initial savings.

1. Vet the Developers Thoroughly: Before committing, assess the developers' skills, experience, and past projects. Look for reviews or testimonials from previous clients.
2. Seek Cultural and Ethical Alignment: Ensure that the outsourcing partner's corporate culture and ethics align with your company. This alignment is crucial for smooth collaboration and mutual understanding.
3. Establish Clear Communication Channels: Set up effective communication channels to ensure regular updates and timely resolution of any issues. This step is crucial for maintaining alignment throughout the project.
4. Implement Quality Assurance Processes: Integrate quality assurance processes early on. Regular code reviews, testing, and adherence to coding standards can significantly improve the final product's quality.
5. Plan for Scope Management: Clearly define the project scope and be vigilant about scope creep. Regular check-ins and project reviews can help keep the project on track.
6. Build a Relationship Beyond Transactions: Foster a relationship with the outsourcing team that transcends mere transactional interactions. Understanding their motivations and challenges can lead to a more productive and committed working relationship.

In conclusion, the quality of developers in outsourced projects cannot be overstated. Companies must strike a balance between cost-efficiency and quality, ensuring that their outsourcing decisions are aligned with long-term business objectives. By focusing on these aspects, companies can mitigate risks associated with outsourcing and harness its full potential for business growth and innovation.

Language & Cultural Difference

The issue of language barriers in outsourced software development is a multifaceted challenge that can significantly impact the efficiency and effectiveness of collaborative efforts. While English is often considered the lingua franca of the global business world, including software development, the reality is that language proficiency varies greatly among outsourced teams. This variation can have profound implications for project outcomes.

Language barriers can hinder the seamless collaboration between product and development teams, which is crucial for the success of any software project. Effective communication is the backbone of Agile methodologies and other collaborative working styles. Misunderstandings or lack of clarity due to language differences can lead to misaligned objectives, improperly implemented features, or even project delays. The nuances of language can affect everything from understanding project requirements to interpreting feedback during the development cycle.

Moreover, language barriers can limit the ability of engineers to participate fully in broader professional communities. This participation is often vital for staying abreast of new technologies, methodologies, and industry best practices. It facilitates the sharing of knowledge and problem-solving techniques, which are essential for continuous professional development and innovation.

While hiring English-speaking resources can mitigate these issues, it often comes at a higher cost. Companies seeking to outsource to regions where English is not the first language may need to invest more to secure team members who are proficient in English. This additional cost needs to be weighed against the benefits of smoother communication and the potential for more effective collaboration.

Even when outsourced teams and in-house teams share a common language, cultural differences in communication styles can lead to misunderstandings. For instance, an American team communicating with counterparts in the UK or Ireland may encounter differences in expressions, accents, or colloquialisms that require clarification. These challenges can be even more pronounced when native languages differ entirely, such as when American teams work with teams whose first languages are Estonian, Hindi, or Spanish. Misinterpretations or the need for repeated clarifications can slow down the development process and lead to frustration on both sides.

In conclusion, language barriers in outsourced software development are a significant concern that requires careful consideration. Companies must acknowledge and proactively manage these challenges through measures such as investing in language training, hiring bilingual project managers, or paying a premium for English-proficient teams. Additionally, fostering an environment of patience and cultural sensitivity can help bridge communication gaps and ensure a more harmonious and productive collaboration between teams from different linguistic backgrounds.

Time Zone Issues

Time zone differences present a significant challenge in outsourced software development, often leading to stress and complications in project management and team collaboration. The impact of these differences is amplified when outsourcing to regions with substantial time differences, such as India or China from the United States, where gaps can range from 13 to 16 hours or more.

One of the primary issues with large time zone differences is the scheduling of meetings and collaborative sessions. When teams are spread across time zones, finding a convenient time for all parties can be challenging. This often results in some team members having to attend meetings late at night or early in the morning, disrupting their work-life balance and potentially affecting their productivity and morale. While short-term adjustments might be manageable, over time, this can lead to burnout, especially for top talent who may have other options where they can work more conventional hours.

Significant time zone gaps can also hinder the vital interaction between product teams and engineering teams. Continuous collaboration and rapid feedback loops are crucial for Agile methodologies and other iterative development processes. When teams cannot work together in real-time, it can slow down decision-making, reduce the effectiveness of brainstorming sessions, and delay the resolution of issues. This lack of synchronicity may lead to prolonged development cycles and can impact the overall quality of the software product.

Moreover, customer interaction and feedback are essential for developing software that truly meets user needs and expectations. Time zone differences can limit opportunities for direct interaction between offshore teams and customers, particularly when immediate feedback or clarification is required. This disconnect can result in misinterpretations of customer requirements or delayed responses to critical feedback.

Emergency situations pose another challenge. When urgent issues arise during the working hours of one region, the offshore team might be unavailable due to the time difference. This can result in delays in addressing critical issues, potentially leading to prolonged system downtimes or other operational disruptions. While some companies attempt to mitigate this by asking developers to work non-standard hours, such an approach is not sustainable in the long term. High-quality developers in competitive markets are likely to seek positions with more reasonable working hours, leading to talent attrition.

Additionally, the twice-yearly time changes in the United States due to Daylight Saving Time can add another layer of complexity to scheduling and coordination with offshore teams. These shifts can disrupt already established schedules and necessitate further adjustments, adding to the overall coordination effort.

To manage these challenges, companies must establish strong processes that can accommodate time zone differences. This might include rotating meeting times to share the inconvenience more equitably, using asynchronous communication methods effectively, and setting clear expectations about availability and response times. Investing in tools that facilitate collaboration across time zones and ensuring that all team members are aware of and respect each other's working hours can also help mitigate some of these challenges. Despite these efforts, however, time zone differences remain a significant hurdle in offshore software development, one that requires careful consideration and ongoing management to ensure project success.

The Crucial Role of Project Planning in Outsourcing

In the realm of outsourced software development, the importance of effective project planning and execution cannot be overstated. The methodologies adopted, such as Agile, play a pivotal role in steering projects towards success. However, these methodologies are often either neglected or misapplied in outsourcing setups, leading to a host of project management challenges.

One of the fundamental issues in outsourcing is the absence of effective planning or the rigid adherence to methodologies that may not suit the dynamic nature of software development. This inflexibility can lead to a variety of problems, including miscommunication, misaligned goals, and an inability to adapt to changing project requirements. Without a solid plan and a flexible approach, projects can quickly become unmanageable, leading to delays, budget overruns, and suboptimal outcomes.

Agile methodologies offer a dynamic and collaborative approach to software development, emphasizing continuous improvement, flexibility, and customer satisfaction. In an outsourcing context, Agile can bridge the gap between different teams and cultures, fostering a shared understanding and a common goal. However, implementing Agile in a distributed team environment requires careful planning, clear communication, and a strong commitment from all parties involved.

Another critical aspect often overlooked in outsourced projects is comprehensive testing and quality assurance. The lack of thorough testing processes can lead to software that is riddled with bugs and performance issues. Addressing these issues post-deployment not only incurs additional costs but can also damage the product's reputation and user satisfaction. Implementing a robust testing and quality assurance framework from the outset is crucial for ensuring the delivery of a high-quality product.

1. Define Clear Objectives and Milestones: Establish clear project objectives, milestones, and deliverables from the start. This clarity helps in aligning the outsourced team with the project's goals.

2. Choose the Right Methodology: Select a project management methodology that aligns with the project's needs and the team's capabilities. Agile, for instance, offers flexibility and continuous feedback, which is beneficial in a dynamic project environment.

3. Ensure Regular Communication: Set up regular meetings and checkpoints to ensure all teams are aligned and any issues are addressed promptly. Effective communication is key to the success of outsourced projects.

4. Incorporate Feedback Loops: Agile methodologies advocate for regular feedback loops. Incorporate these feedback mechanisms to continually refine and improve the project outcomes.

5. Invest in Quality Assurance: Allocate resources for thorough testing and quality assurance throughout the project lifecycle. This investment pays off in the form of a more reliable and user-friendly product.

6. Adapt and Evolve: Be prepared to adapt the plan as the project progresses. Flexibility is crucial in responding to unforeseen challenges and changes in project requirements.

Effective project planning and execution are the cornerstones of successful software outsourcing. By prioritizing clear objectives, adopting suitable methodologies, emphasizing communication, and focusing on quality assurance, companies can greatly enhance the chances of their outsourced projects' success. These strategies not only ensure smoother project execution but also pave the way for building long-term, productive relationships with outsourcing partners.

Mitigating the Risk from Vendor Lock

Vendor lock-in is a significant concern in the realm of software development outsourcing. It occurs when a company becomes heavily reliant on a single external vendor for critical development tasks, creating a dependency that can be risky and difficult to break. This situation often arises when a vendor fails to deliver, underperforms, or, in worse cases, goes out of business. The challenge is compounded by the fact that transitioning to a different provider can be a costly and complex process, involving significant time and resource investments.

One of the key problems with vendor lock-in is the stifling effect it can have on a company's flexibility and innovation. Being tied to a specific vendor's technologies and methodologies can limit the company's ability to negotiate effectively due to the high costs and complexities involved in switching providers. This reliance can also hinder the company from exploring competitive pricing options and new, innovative solutions offered by other providers in the market.

To tackle these challenges, companies can adopt several strategies. Engaging multiple vendors for different aspects of the software development process is a prudent approach to reduce reliance on any single provider. This not only diversifies risks but also encourages competitive pricing and service quality. Opting for standardized technologies and platforms, rather than vendor-specific solutions, can facilitate easier transitions to new providers if needed. It ensures the skills required for the project are more universally available, thus reducing dependency on a single vendor's expertise.

The role of clear contractual agreements is paramount. These should include comprehensive clauses for knowledge transfer, documentation standards, and contingency plans in case of vendor failure, outlining terms for ending the relationship, including the handover of code, documentation, and other essential data.

Developing in-house expertise in crucial areas of the software development process can also mitigate the risks associated with vendor lock-in. By fostering internal skills and knowledge, companies can maintain greater control over projects and facilitate smoother transitions if a change in vendor becomes necessary.

Regular performance reviews of the vendor's work against agreed-upon benchmarks and standards help identify potential issues early on. This proactive approach allows for timely adjustments and decisions regarding the continuation or termination of the vendor relationship. Moreover, having a well-thought-out exit strategy, including data and code retrieval processes and alternative vendor options, provides a safety net and ensures preparedness for any eventuality, such as vendor underperformance or the need to switch providers.

In essence, navigating the risks of vendor lock-in in software development outsourcing requires strategic planning, diversified vendor engagement, standardization, and building internal competencies. These measures collectively ensure more resilient and flexible software development operations, safeguarding the company from potential pitfalls associated with over-reliance on a single external provider.

A Special Note about Working with Talent in Warzones

This book does not purport to have the answers or experience working with outsourcing partners that are in an area of active military combat, but given the amount of software development that is outsourced to Ukraine, or another region with active military conflicts, it's something that needs to be included in the calculation and is a real concern for companies. It may even prevent some companies from considering outsourcing.

When considering Ukraine as a destination for outsourced software development, it's important to recognize the context in which these developers have been operating, particularly prior to the onset of Russia's military action. Ukraine has become a hub for tech talent and innovation, gaining recognition as a leading outsourcing destination due to its skilled developers, cultural proximity to Western countries, and competitive pricing.

Working with Ukrainian developers often meant tapping into a pool of talent well-versed in a range of technologies and programming languages. Ukrainian developers were known for their strong technical education, problem-solving skills, and a good command of English, which facilitated communication with international clients. The Ukrainian IT sector had developed a robust infrastructure for remote collaboration, with a focus on Agile methodologies and modern project management practices.

Before the conflict, companies valued Ukrainian outsourced teams for their ability to work within European time zones, making real-time collaboration more feasible. Additionally, there was a cultural affinity, particularly with European countries, which helped in aligning work styles and expectations. Ukrainian developers were also adept at integrating into existing teams, bringing fresh perspectives and a strong work ethic to projects.

However, the situation has since changed dramatically due to the conflict. Organizations looking to work with Ukrainian developers must now consider a myriad of factors, including the safety and well-being of their outsourced teams, potential disruptions due to the conflict, and the overall stability of their operations. It's crucial to maintain open lines of communication with Ukrainian partners, offering support and flexibility as they navigate these challenges.

Furthermore, companies must be prepared for contingencies, including potential relocation of their Ukrainian team members or providing assistance with remote work setups if developers are displaced. The focus should be on creating a sustainable working environment that accounts for the well-being of all team members while ensuring that project deliverables can still be met.

In conclusion, working with outsourced developers from Ukraine, given the current context, requires a deep sense of empathy, a commitment to the partnership beyond the transactional relationship, and a readiness to adapt to rapidly changing circumstances. It's about building a resilient collaboration that can withstand the pressures of geopolitical instability while continuing to foster innovation and growth.

Relationship Management with Outsourcing Agency

The relationship between a company and its outsourcing agency is a critical component that significantly influences the outcome of a project. The nature of this relationship extends far beyond a simple client-vendor transaction; it encapsulates a partnership that can drive the project towards success or lead to its downfall.

One of the common pitfalls in outsourcing arrangements is the perception of the outsourcing agency as merely a service provider, rather than an integral part of the team. This viewpoint can create a psychological and professional divide, fostering an environment of detachment rather than collaboration. To maximize the potential of an outsourcing partnership, it is essential to integrate the agency into the team, valuing their input and treating them as equal stakeholders in the project's success.

Outsourcing agencies often bring a wealth of knowledge and experience, having worked on diverse projects across different domains. By not tapping into this reservoir of expertise, companies may miss out on innovative ideas and improvement opportunities that could significantly enhance their project. Engaging actively with the outsourcing partner, seeking their advice, and involving them in key decision-making processes can uncover new perspectives and solutions that internal teams might overlook.

1. Open Communication: Establish clear and open lines of communication. Encourage regular interactions not just on operational aspects but also on strategic levels to ensure alignment of goals and expectations.
2. Joint Planning Sessions: Involve the outsourcing team in planning sessions. Their insights can offer valuable inputs for refining project strategies and execution plans.
3. Feedback Mechanisms: Implement a two-way feedback system where both parties can openly discuss improvements, concerns, and compliments. This approach fosters a culture of continuous improvement and mutual respect.
4. Cultural Sensitivity: Acknowledge and respect cultural differences. Understanding each other's work culture and norms can greatly enhance interpersonal dynamics and team cohesiveness.
5. Shared Vision and Goals: Work towards establishing a shared vision and common goals. When the outsourcing partner is attuned to the company's broader objectives, they are more likely to go the extra mile to achieve success.
6. Recognition and Incentives: Acknowledge the contributions of the outsourcing team and consider incentives for exceptional performance. Recognition can significantly boost morale and commitment to the project.

By transforming the traditional client-vendor relationship into a strategic partnership, companies can leverage the full potential of their outsourcing arrangements. This paradigm shift not only enhances project outcomes but also paves the way for long-term collaborations that can yield substantial benefits for both parties.

Effective relationship management in outsourcing is about building partnerships, fostering collaboration, and leveraging collective expertise for mutual benefit. By nurturing a relationship that transcends the conventional boundaries of client-vendor dynamics, companies can unlock new avenues for innovation, efficiency, and growth, ultimately leading to the successful realization of their software development goals.

Navigating Intellectual Property Challenges in Outsourcing

In the realm of software development and technological innovation, outsourcing has become a common strategy for companies aiming to optimize efficiency, reduce costs, and leverage external expertise. However, this approach is not without its risks, particularly concerning the protection of intellectual property (IP) rights. This article aims to explore effective strategies for safeguarding IP during outsourcing engagements.

Intellectual property rights are vital for safeguarding the creations of the mind, ranging from software codes and artistic works to inventions and brand identities. These rights are not only central to the economic value of a firm but also to its competitive edge in the market. Therefore, sharing intellectual property with external vendors, as often happens in outsourcing, necessitates a robust strategy to mitigate associated risks.

Copyrights: Protect creative works, including software code, website content, and artistic creations. They last for the author's lifetime plus 70 years in the U.S.

Patents: Guard innovations and improvements in technology, including software functionalities. They typically last for 20 years.

Trademarks: Defend brand identities like logos, business names, or slogans. Renewal is required every 10 years in the U.S.

Trade Secrets: Protect non-public business information, ranging from technical data to strategic plans.

Industrial Designs: Shield the aesthetic aspects of products, including their shape, pattern, or color.

Outsourcing your software development involves sharing potentially sensitive IP with external partners. This section delves into six critical steps to protect your IP in such scenarios:

1. Due Diligence: Before engaging with an outsourcing vendor, conduct thorough research on their reputation, past IP breaches, and internal risk measures. Evaluate their legal standing and operational processes, including their approach to subcontracting.

2. Non-Disclosure Agreements (NDAs): An essential first step is signing an NDA with your outsourcing partner. This legal document should clearly outline the scope of confidentiality and extend beyond the duration of your business relationship.

3. Adherence to Legal Frameworks: Understand and utilize the IP protection laws applicable in your country and the vendor's country. Ensure your agreements reflect these legal standards and offer enforceable remedies in case of a breach.

4. Comprehensive Master Service Agreements: These agreements should detail service delivery terms, intellectual property ownership, dispute resolution mechanisms, and data protection strategies. Clarify the ownership of the final work product and the rights associated with its use and modification.

5. Understanding Vendor Processes: Inquire about the vendor's project management tools, data storage practices, security measures for sensitive information, and policies for employee access to company resources.

6. Limited Access and Transition Protocols: Restrict vendor access to your server and data, allowing only what's necessary for their work. Store all source codes and applications on your company's servers and use platforms like GitHub for secure storage.

To further ensure the security of your intellectual property, consider asking your outsourcing vendor the following questions:

- How do they maintain confidentiality and data security?

- What measures are in place for secure information transfer and storage?

- How do they manage IP rights transfer effectively?

Outsourcing offers a spectrum of benefits but also brings challenges, particularly regarding intellectual property. By understanding the types of IP rights, conducting thorough due diligence, establishing legal safeguards through NDAs and service agreements, and consistently monitoring and limiting data access, companies can effectively mitigate the risks associated with IP leakage. These steps, coupled with a clear understanding and negotiation of IP terms with your outsourcing partner, are crucial in protecting your company's most valuable assets in an increasingly interconnected digital landscape.

Successfully navigating the complexities of software development outsourcing demands a comprehensive understanding of these challenges. Companies need to establish clear, realistic expectations, maintain effective communication, and cultivate a collaborative relationship with their outsourcing partners. By addressing these aspects thoughtfully, businesses can effectively mitigate risks and maximize the benefits of global talent in achieving their software development objectives.

Addressing Cybersecurity in Outsourcing Software Development

In the realm of outsourcing software development, cybersecurity emerges as a pivotal concern. This section of the book is dedicated to understanding and mitigating the cybersecurity risks associated with outsourcing. It's crucial to recognize that when you outsource software development, the responsibility for cybersecurity extends beyond your immediate organization.

The first step in this process involves revising your existing cybersecurity policies and procedures to incorporate the outsourced team. This means ensuring that the outsourced staff complies with any background checks or security procedures that your frameworks demand. Such a practice is not only about adherence to protocols but also about maintaining a uniform security standard across both in-house and outsourced teams.

A key aspect of cybersecurity in outsourcing is managing data access, especially in the context of compliance requirements. For instance, organizations under the FedRAMP compliance regime must be careful not to grant access to their production systems to foreign nationals. This highlights the importance of understanding and strictly adhering to compliance requirements when outsourcing software development.

Outsourcing also means an expanded scope of your IT infrastructure. You are faced with a choice: either get the outsourced firm to implement your security controls and tools or ensure they take actions that align with your compliance requirements. This might include extending your IT infrastructure to their endpoints and servers, which can introduce new vulnerabilities.

Incorporating your DevSecOps tools into the outsourced firm's infrastructure is another critical step. This integration may have implications for licensing and may require negotiations to install necessary software on the contractors' machines. Such an extension is crucial for maintaining consistent security practices across all development and operational activities.

Equally important is the training of all personnel, particularly those with access to production data. This is especially crucial in environments that need to comply with frameworks like PCI or ISO 27001, as any oversight could lead to data breaches and an expanded risk footprint.

Collaborating closely with your Chief Information Security Officer (CISO) is essential. This partnership ensures that the strategic onboarding of outsourced firms is aligned with your overarching cybersecurity strategy. Such collaboration is vital for continual improvement in cybersecurity practices.

Selecting reliable vendors and developers is another cornerstone of cybersecurity in outsourcing. It's important to partner with entities known for their secure software development practices. This includes researching their reputation, past performance, and compliance with relevant security certifications. Transparent communication about security practices and policies is crucial, as is the use of digital signatures in contracts to ensure data security and intellectual property rights. Control over user access should be stringent, adhering to the least privilege principle.

Navigating cybersecurity in outsourcing software development is a multifaceted challenge that requires a balanced approach. By updating cybersecurity practices, managing compliance, expanding infrastructure security, and ensuring thorough training, organizations can mitigate the inherent risks of outsourcing. Additionally, a close collaboration with the CISO and careful selection of vendors and developers will bolster the security measures. While risks are an inherent part of outsourcing, with the right strategies and vigilant management, these can be effectively controlled, allowing organizations to reap the benefits of outsourcing while maintaining robust cybersecurity.

Navigating Software Licensing in Outsourcing Partnerships

In the realm of software development outsourcing, managing software licenses is a crucial yet often overlooked aspect. This section delves into the practicalities of handling software licenses in an outsourcing scenario, highlighting the responsibilities and considerations for both the client and the outsourcing firm.

Software licenses are legal instruments governing the use of various software tools and platforms. These licenses can range from development environments and code libraries to design tools and project management software. In an outsourcing setup, clarity on who holds and manages these licenses is essential to ensure seamless operations and legal compliance.

The Shared Responsibility of Software Licenses

1. Outsourcing Firm's Licenses: Many outsourcing companies come equipped with their own set of licenses for common development tools and platforms. This is particularly beneficial for clients as it reduces the overhead of acquiring and managing these licenses. These firms often have enterprise agreements that allow them to extend the usage of these tools to their client projects.

2. Client-Purchased Licenses: In some cases, especially when specialized or proprietary software is involved, the client might need to provide licenses to the outsourcing team. This scenario often occurs when the software in question is specific to the client's business or when there are legal or compliance reasons that mandate the client's direct control over the software licenses.

Key Considerations in License Management

- Compliance with Licensing Agreements: Ensuring that all software used in the development process complies with the respective licensing agreements is critical. This includes adhering to the terms regarding the number of users, usage scope, and geographical limitations.

- Cost Implications: Understanding who bears the cost of the licenses is a vital part of the contractual agreement between the client and the outsourcing firm. Clients should factor in these costs when calculating the overall budget for the outsourcing project.

- Access and Control: In scenarios where the client provides licenses, there should be clear mechanisms for granting and revoking access to these software tools. This control is crucial for maintaining security and managing resource allocation effectively.

- License Audits and Renewals: Regular audits of software licenses can prevent lapses and ensure that all tools are up-to-date and in compliance. Both parties should be aware of renewal dates and changes in licensing terms to avoid disruption in the development process.

An effective approach to software licensing in outsourcing relationships involves a collaborative strategy. For instance, an outsourcing firm might use its own licensed development environments and collaboration tools, while the client provides licenses for specialized software that is central to their business operations. This synergy allows for cost-effective and compliant use of necessary software, benefiting both parties.

Navigating the intricacies of software licenses in outsourcing arrangements requires a clear understanding, meticulous planning, and open communication between the client and the outsourcing firm. By collaboratively determining the responsibility for software licenses and ensuring adherence to licensing terms, companies can maintain legal compliance, optimize costs, and ensure that the necessary tools are available for the successful completion of the project.

State of Outsourcing Today

The software development outsourcing industry is a major source of global trade, and growing. This section explores the current state of the industry, the players, the customers, and the hotspot regions.

Size of Application Outsourcing Industry

The application outsourcing industry has witnessed a consistent increase in revenue over the years, signaling a robust and expanding market. Starting from $97.65 billion in 2016, there has been a notable year-on-year growth, reaching projections of $129.90 billion by 2028.

This growth reflects the escalating demand for specialized application services that span various business functions and industries. Companies are increasingly turning to outsourcing to drive innovation, tap into advanced technological capabilities, and enhance their competitive edge. This trend is fueled by the need to address rapidly changing market demands, digitize traditional business models, and manage complex application landscapes more efficiently.

With application outsourcing forming a significant portion of the IT outsourcing sector, businesses are leveraging external expertise to not only cut costs but also to accelerate time-to-market for new software products and updates. The rising revenue figures are indicative of the trust and investment that businesses place in outsourcing partners to deliver critical software solutions that align with strategic business objectives.

This upward trajectory also points to a maturing market where outsourcing firms are expected to provide not just labor arbitrage but strategic value-adds such as agile development practices, robust security protocols, and innovation-driven approaches. As companies worldwide continue to embrace digital transformation, the application outsourcing industry is poised to play a pivotal role in shaping the future of software development and business technology.

Offshore vs Nearshore vs Onshore Models

The current state of outsourcing reveals a dynamic interplay between nearshore, offshore, and onshore models, each serving distinct needs and preferences of businesses globally. The attached image, which presents data up until December 2023, showcases a clear trend in the distribution of outsourcing revenue by type.

In 2020, onshore outsourcing dominated the market share with 36.96%, closely followed by offshore at 47.63%, and nearshore at 15.41% (Statista). This initial distribution indicates a strong preference for outsourcing within the same country or region, possibly due to cultural alignment and ease of communication. However, offshore outsourcing held a significant portion, highlighting the cost benefits and access to a global talent pool that companies seek.

As we move forward in time, there is a noticeable increase in the nearshore segment, climbing steadily to 24.97% by 2028. This growth can be attributed to companies looking to combine the benefits of cultural and geographical proximity with cost savings. Nearshore outsourcing has become particularly appealing for businesses looking to maintain more control over projects with the added advantage of similar time zones, which facilitates real-time collaboration.

Offshore outsourcing remains substantial but shows a slight decline in percentage terms, potentially due to businesses' concerns over data security, intellectual property rights, and the complexities of managing projects across vast time zones. Nevertheless, with a projected market share of 45.24% by 2028, offshore outsourcing continues to be a significant player, underlining its enduring appeal for cost-effectiveness and scalability.

Onshore outsourcing exhibits a gradual decrease in market share, dropping to 29.78% by 2028. This could reflect the evolving nature of businesses that are increasingly comfortable with managing distant teams or perhaps a push towards more cost-effective solutions that nearshore and offshore options represent.

The data suggests a strategic shift in how companies are outsourcing, with a notable rise in nearshore services as they seek a balance between the benefits of onshore proximity and the cost advantages of offshore resources. Despite the market impacts of the Russia-Ukraine war and other geopolitical factors, businesses are adapting their outsourcing strategies to navigate the complexities of the global market. This adaptability is crucial in leveraging the strengths of each model to optimize operational efficiency, reduce costs, and enhance competitive advantage in an increasingly digital world.

Industries that Outsource

The outsourcing landscape is diverse, with various industries leveraging external expertise to enhance their operations. The graph for the year ending December 2023 delineates the revenue share by industry in the outsourcing market, providing a clear picture of who is outsourcing their processes.

The Banking, Financial Services, and Insurance (BFSI) sector is the most prominent player in outsourcing, accounting for a significant 30.29% of the industry's revenue. This substantial share underscores the sector's reliance on outsourcing for a range of functions from back-end operations to customer service and IT solutions, driven by the need for cost optimization, improved operational efficiency, and access to advanced technologies.

Healthcare follows closely, constituting 23.43% of the market revenue. Outsourcing in healthcare is primarily motivated by the need for specialized expertise in IT solutions, patient data management, and regulatory compliance, highlighting the sector's push towards digital transformation and improved patient care through technological integration.

IT & Telecom industries also rely heavily on outsourcing, making up

15.77% of the revenue share. These sectors outsource to keep up with rapid technological advancements, manage complex infrastructures, and cater to the growing demand for innovative products and services.

Manufacturing represents 12.57% of the revenue, indicating its ongoing strategy to outsource to manage supply chain complexities, optimize production costs, and innovate product development through external technological aid.

Retail and Wholesale sectors account for 11.43%, showing a strategic use of outsourcing to manage e-commerce platforms, customer relations, inventory systems, and to stay competitive in a rapidly evolving retail landscape.

The 'Others' category, comprising 6.51%, includes industries like education, media, and utilities, which are increasingly turning to outsourcing to modernize operations and adopt new technologies to enhance service delivery and customer engagement.

This revenue distribution highlights a clear trend: industries across the board are increasingly turning to outsourcing not only as a cost-saving measure but also as a strategic tool to access specialized skills, improve service quality, and stay agile in a fast-paced global economy. As industries continue to evolve and digitalization becomes imperative, the reliance on outsourcing is likely to expand, with industries seeking to capitalize on the benefits it offers in a bid to stay competitive and relevant.

The outsourcing industry is highly fragmented, with numerous players competing for market share. However, a few notable companies have established themselves as leaders. According to the chart for 2022, Accenture leads the pack with an 8% share in the outsourcing market, distinguishing itself as a heavyweight in providing comprehensive outsourcing services, from IT strategy to operations and implementation.

Following Accenture, Hitachi claims a 5% share, showcasing its robust capabilities in IT and digital transformation services. Capgemini and Kyndryl each hold a 4% share, reflecting their strong global presence and full-service portfolios that address a wide range of outsourcing needs across various sectors.

Cognizant and Fujitsu are not far behind, each with a 3% share, indicating their competitive edge in providing technology and business process services. Infosys, NTT Data, and Tata Consultancy Services (TCS) each have secured a 2% market share, pointing to their role as key players in the industry, particularly noted for their offshore capabilities and contributions to the global delivery model.

Smaller percentages are held by companies such as SAIC and Samsung SD, each with 1%, underscoring their niche offerings and strategic positioning in the market. The vast majority of the market, however, is represented by a diverse array of other companies, collectively accounting for 59%. This diversity reflects a market teeming with specialized providers catering to a broad spectrum of outsourcing needs, from niche technology solutions to comprehensive service offerings.

This landscape signifies not only the competitive nature of the outsourcing industry but also the vast opportunities for businesses to find partners that align with their specific needs. Whether it's embracing new technologies, entering new markets, or driving operational efficiency, these leading companies demonstrate the potential to be strategic partners in transformation and innovation for businesses globally.

Geographic Leaders

The global outsourcing industry is a dynamic and significant sector, with several regions around the world emerging as powerhouses due to their large market sizes and growth potential.

India stands as a titan in the industry with an expected market size of

$210 billion by 2025, up from $150 billion in 2020. The country's annual growth rate is projected at 7.25%, demonstrating India's continued dominance and expertise in outsourcing, particularly in IT and software development services.

The Philippines is also a prominent player, with its market size projected to grow from $26 billion in 2020 to $40 billion by 2025, at an impressive compound annual growth rate (CAGR) of 9.8%. This growth underscores the country's strong reputation in customer support and business process outsourcing, fueled by a highly skilled, English-speaking workforce.

Southeast Asia is not far behind, with a collective market size that is expected to increase from $23 billion in 2020 to $47 billion by 2025, growing at a CAGR of 8.5%. This region, encompassing countries like Thailand, Vietnam, and Malaysia, is known for its burgeoning digital marketing, business support operations, and IT outsourcing services.

China, with its vast manufacturing capabilities, is anticipated to see its market size swell from $40 billion in 2020 to $52 billion by 2025, growing at a CAGR of 6.2%. China's role in the outsourcing industry is supported by its robust infrastructure, cost-effectiveness, and large-scale production capacity.

Eastern Europe is another significant region in the outsourcing landscape, projected to reach a market size of $31 billion by 2025 from $32 billion in 2020, with a CAGR of 6.8%. Countries like Ukraine, Poland, and Romania are particularly noted for their high-quality software development and IT services, combined with competitive cost advantages.

These regions represent a diverse and thriving outsourcing industry that offers a wide array of services and benefits. Companies across the globe leverage these markets for their competitive advantages in costs, skilled labor pools, and growing technological capabilities, making them pivotal in the global business strategy for outsourcing.

Finding Talent

In an increasingly competitive global market, the hunt for skilled technical talent is becoming a significant hurdle for many companies. A ManpowerGroup survey reflects this challenge starkly, with 77% of employers reporting difficulties in finding the right talent to fulfill their technical requirements. This scarcity is not just about numbers; it's about the depth of skill and expertise required in a technology-driven business landscape.

This talent gap has far-reaching implications. It can stunt growth, delay product development, and hinder a company's ability to innovate and stay ahead of the curve. In response, businesses are looking beyond traditional hiring methods to bridge this gap. Upskilling current employees is one strategy being adopted, investing in training and development to elevate the existing workforce's capabilities to meet the evolving demands of their roles.

However, upskilling is only a part of the solution. Many companies are turning to global IT outsourcing as a strategic move to access a broader talent pool. Outsourcing can offer a dual benefit—tapping into a global reservoir of specialized skills and potentially reducing costs associated with hiring and training. By doing so, companies are not only filling immediate technical needs but are also positioning themselves for long-term success by securing a pipeline of capable and adaptable talent.

As we enter 2024, the reliance on outsourcing as a viable solution to the talent crunch is likely to grow. For companies, this means not only finding the right outsourcing partner but also building a collaborative relationship that extends beyond a mere transactional interaction. It's about creating a synergy where outsourced teams are seen as an extension of the in-house team, contributing not just their technical expertise but also participating in a shared vision for innovation and growth.

Navigating this aspect of workforce management will require a delicate balance of internal development and external sourcing, ensuring that investments in people—whether in-house or outsourced—align with the strategic objectives of the company.

Supply & Demand of Skill Sets

In the rapidly evolving landscape of IT outsourcing, the equilibrium between supply and demand for various technical skill sets is a crucial factor for businesses to consider. As depicted in the visual graph, there is a varied landscape of talent availability versus market need across different IT specializations.

Front-end development showcases a high supply meeting high demand. This indicates a healthy market where there is a balance between the number of skilled professionals and the number of opportunities available. The proliferation of web technologies and the continuous need for more interactive and sophisticated user interfaces drive this demand.

In contrast, the domain of Machine Learning and Data Science is marked by high demand but lower supply. This reflects the current industry trend where the need for advanced analytical skills and the ability to create data-driven AI solutions outstrips the availability of qualified professionals. Companies looking to outsource these skills may face stiffer competition for talent and potentially higher costs due to the scarcity.

Mobile development, although not as scarce as Machine Learning and Data Science, still shows a higher demand relative to supply. With the ongoing shift towards mobile-first strategies in many businesses, mobile developers, particularly those proficient in both Android and iOS platforms, are in high demand.

In terms of Infrastructure & Cloud services, the graph indicates that the supply is moderate relative to the market demand. With cloud solutions becoming a standard for business operations, professionals with expertise in cloud infrastructure are needed to ensure scalable, secure, and cost-effective computing environments.

The area of Test & Quality Assurance exhibits a somewhat high supply when compared to demand. Despite this, the critical role of QA in software development ensures a steady need for these professionals to maintain the high standards of software performance and reliability.

Embedded & Application development is marked by a low supply and demand, which might suggest a niche market. These specialties often require deep technical expertise in specific areas, such as IoT device development or specific application types, and might not be as widely sought after as more mainstream IT skills.

This supply-demand dynamic presents opportunities and challenges. Companies may find it easier to source certain skills but may need to invest more in securing top talent in areas where the demand outstrips supply. Furthermore, it underscores the importance of fostering a strong pipeline of talent and possibly investing in training and development to bridge any skill gaps.

Growth Expectations

In the current business landscape, organizations are continually evaluating their outsourcing strategies to align with their evolving operational needs and market dynamics. The provided data suggests a significant trend in the industry's future direction.

Approximately half of the organizations, at 49.6%, are planning to increase their outsourcing activities. This substantial proportion indicates a strong confidence in the benefits of outsourcing, such as cost reduction, access to specialized skills, and the ability to focus on core business competencies.

Conversely, a smaller segment, 10.4%, plans to reduce their reliance on outsourcing. This group may be looking to consolidate their operations, bring skills in-house, or may have faced challenges with outsourcing that they are now seeking to rectify through other means.

Meanwhile, a substantial 40% of organizations plan to maintain their current level of outsourcing. These companies may have found a balance that suits their current business model, or they may be taking a cautious approach to changing market conditions.

Overall, the data reflects a dynamic environment where a significant number of organizations are recognizing the strategic value of outsourcing and are either maintaining or increasing their commitment to it. This trend underscores the importance of outsourcing as a key component of modern business strategy, offering flexibility and scalability to adapt to changing market demands and technological advancements.

(Statistics provided in this section are from Statista)

Outsourcing Is Changing

As with other growing industries, the state of play is continuously changing. This section explores a few of the changes affecting software outsourcing today.

Providers Are Becoming Customers

As the global landscape of outsourcing continues to evolve, two countries that have been synonymous with the supply of outsourced software talent are witnessing a paradigm shift. China and India, traditionally known as the powerhouses of the outsourcing industry, are now experiencing burgeoning domestic demands for IT services, reflecting their rapid economic growth and diversification.

China's remarkable economic expansion has been accompanied by a digital transformation across its industrial sectors. This has spurred an internal demand for software development and IT services, as companies within China seek to innovate and integrate advanced technologies into their operations. The Chinese government's support for technological advancement has further fueled this demand, with a focus on developing a robust domestic IT infrastructure and services sector.

India, often referred to as the "world's back office," has long been the go-to destination for software development and IT outsourcing due to its vast pool of English-speaking IT professionals and competitive pricing. However, with its economy growing and diversifying, there is an increasing appetite for these services within the country itself. Indian businesses are increasingly leveraging technology for competitive advantage, resulting in a significant uptick in demand for IT talent to serve the local market.

Both countries are also seeing a surge in technology startups and digital entrepreneurship, which is contributing to the domestic demand for software and IT services. As these startups scale and the domestic market grows, the need for IT expertise is further accentuated.

This shift is not only changing the dynamics of the global outsourcing market but also impacting the availability of talent for international clients. As China and India continue to harness their IT capabilities to fuel domestic growth, the global outsourcing landscape may see a redistribution of talent, with these nations moving up the value chain from being just outsourcing destinations to becoming significant end-users of IT services.

Rates are Normalizing Globally

The world of software development outsourcing is undergoing a significant transformation, particularly in the realm of cost. Not so long ago, there was a stark contrast between the rates charged by software developers in the United States compared to those in countries like China or India. The landscape, however, is swiftly changing, and the gap in outsourcing rates is narrowing.

A decade back, the average normalized rate for an Indian offshore development team hovered around $15 per hour—a figure that factored in various skill levels within the team, from junior developers to architects and leads. Now, that rate has escalated to approximately $40 per hour, aligning more closely with what one might expect to pay for teams in Eastern Europe or South America.

This leveling of rates is largely due to the global nature of work today. As technology has advanced, it has become increasingly feasible for work to be conducted from virtually anywhere in the world, allowing for a more fluid distribution of IT services. This globalization has led to a certain homogenization of rates; there is less variance in what companies can expect to pay for software development talent across different regions.

While there remains a premium on talent in tech hubs like Silicon Valley, the disparity is not as pronounced when comparing developers from less costly regions of the U.S., such as Alabama or West Virginia, to those from Poland, Argentina, or Malaysia. This suggests a trend towards a more unified global market rate for software development, where geographical location is becoming less of a determining factor in cost. Companies are finding that investing in talent is less about finding the lowest rate and more about securing the best value for their investment, regardless of where that talent is located.

This shift towards rate normalization presents both opportunities and challenges. On one hand, companies can access a wider talent pool without the constraints of significant cost differences. On the other, competition for top-tier talent intensifies as more organizations vie for the best developers, regardless of their physical location. As this trend continues, companies may find that their location no longer offers the cost advantage it once did, prompting a reevaluation of outsourcing strategies and an increased focus on value-driven rather than cost-driven hiring decisions.

Enter Africa

The global outsourcing landscape is witnessing an emerging trend with Africa becoming a significant player in the IT outsourcing market. As broadband internet becomes more widespread across the continent and educational institutions modernize their curricula to meet global standards, Africa is positioning itself as an attractive destination for software development services.

This burgeoning market is characterized by a dynamic and increasingly skilled workforce, bolstered by the continent's efforts to embrace technological advancements and improve digital literacy. African countries are making concerted efforts to provide robust IT education, with universities revamping their programs to include the latest in software development and data science, thereby producing graduates ready to meet the demands of the global IT sector.

The perception of Africa as a continent offering only low-cost outsourcing solutions is changing. While countries like Egypt, Morocco, and Kenya offer competitive rates—often around $20 or less per hour for offshore programming roles—others like Nigeria and South Africa are emerging as higher-value destinations. In these countries, the average rates for hiring software developers can range between $40 to $50, indicative of the growing expertise and experience found within their talent pools.

It's important for businesses seeking to outsource to not merely view Africa as a monolith but as a diverse continent with a wide range of outsourcing potentials. Each country has its unique offerings in terms of cost, expertise, and experience. South Africa, for instance, with its advanced infrastructure and higher rates, is indicative of a market that is maturing rapidly and offering more sophisticated IT services.

As the continent continues to improve its connectivity and educational frameworks, the potential for growth in the African IT outsourcing sector is vast. This shift provides an opportunity for global businesses to tap into a new and enthusiastic market, while also contributing to the development of the IT industry in Africa. As more companies recognize the value of African developers, the continent is poised to become a key hub in the global IT outsourcing ecosystem, characterized by a balanced mix of affordability and quality.

AI

Artificial Intelligence (AI) is swiftly transforming the IT outsourcing industry, fundamentally altering the development process from the ground up. Tools imbued with AI, such as GitHub's Copilot, are supercharging developer productivity, with estimates suggesting a productivity boost of up to 50%. These innovations allow developers to devote more attention to complex problems rather than mundane coding tasks. Outsourcing firms are recognizing the need to adapt, with a focus on reskilling their workforce to align with the changing demand for AI-driven development skills over traditional business logic and machine learning.

The rise of low-code and no-code platforms is another significant trend influenced by AI, enabling individuals without extensive programming knowledge to create their own applications. This democratization of development is likely to alter the nature of outsourcing engagements, shifting the focus towards empowering end-users.

AI's influence extends to automating routine software development tasks, such as code formatting and preliminary debugging, thus freeing up developers to invest more time in innovation. Moreover, AI is accelerating the development cycle by enabling automated code generation for websites and applications, which translates into faster product launches.

In data analytics, AI excels at processing and analyzing large volumes of data, uncovering insights that lead to informed decision-making and enhanced development strategies. The quality assurance processes have also been bolstered by AI algorithms that meticulously scan for code inconsistencies and potential errors, ensuring software products meet high-quality standards and deliver satisfactory user experiences.

From a cost perspective, AI's automation capabilities are generating significant savings and offering scalable solutions that adapt to project demands. This scalability is particularly advantageous in automated testing and debugging, where AI's precision and speed in error detection streamline the process, cutting down on deployment time and elevating the end product's reliability.

Customer support services have been revolutionized by AI through the deployment of intelligent chatbots that can instantly and accurately respond to customer queries, providing a seamless support experience. Furthermore, AI is aiding developers in optimizing software performance by identifying and resolving bottlenecks, which results in more efficient and effective applications.

Efficiency gains are not confined to development alone; they also permeate project management. AI-driven tools are adept at handling complex scheduling, resource allocation, and risk assessment, fostering a collaborative environment that leads to more successful project outcomes.

AI is enhancing the security aspect of web development as well, automating the detection of and response to security threats, thereby minimizing human error and fortifying the security protocols of software products.

In summary, AI is not simply facilitating but revolutionizing the IT outsourcing field, driving efficiencies, enhancing quality, and fostering innovation. This shift is prompting businesses to seek outsourcing partners that are not merely service providers but are at the forefront of employing AI to deliver cutting-edge products and services. As AI continues to permeate the industry, it becomes clear that the future of outsourcing will be defined by those who can seamlessly integrate AI into their service offerings.

The Rise of Remote Work

The normalization of remote work has ushered in a paradigm shift in corporate operations, making outsourcing a more seamless and integrated process. In an era where work from home has become a staple, the geographical location of team members has become increasingly irrelevant. This shift has significant implications for outsourcing, as it dismantles the traditional barriers of distance and time zones that once complicated such arrangements.

With ubiquitous digital communication tools such as Zoom and Microsoft Teams becoming daily fixtures in professional lives, the distinction between a coworker located in a bustling city like Boston and another in the vibrant streets of Buenos Aires has diminished. The playing field has been leveled, with the same set of tools enabling real-time collaboration, regardless of physical location. This accessibility to a global workforce is particularly advantageous to companies looking to outsource, as it widens the talent pool while maintaining operational cohesiveness.

Moreover, the proliferation of cloud-based technologies and collaborative platforms has enabled a smooth transition to remote work, ensuring that all team members, whether in-house or outsourced, can contribute effectively. The digital infrastructure that supports remote work—from shared drives to project management software— has been integral in facilitating this transition. It allows teams to share files, track progress, and maintain productivity without the need for a centralized office space.

This shift to remote work has not only made outsourcing more viable but has also encouraged a more inclusive approach to team integration. Remote work policies have necessitated the development of robust virtual communication protocols, which are equally applicable to both local and outsourced team members. As a result, companies are now more equipped than ever to incorporate outsourced professionals into their workflows as seamlessly as if they were located in the office next door.

In conclusion, the normalization of remote work has indeed been a game-changer for the outsourcing industry. It has not only simplified the process of integrating outsourced teams but has also reinforced the notion that the efficacy of collaboration is not contingent on physical proximity. This realization opens up a world of possibilities for businesses to innovate, expand, and operate with unprecedented agility and diversity in their workforce.

Micro-Outsourcing

The advent of micro-outsourcing signifies a paradigm shift in the domain of IT outsourcing, characterized by the delegation of discrete, specialized tasks to external teams, as opposed to the traditional model of outsourcing entire projects. This granular approach to outsourcing offers heightened flexibility and precision in engaging external expertise, aligning closely with specific project needs.

Micro-outsourcing emerges as a strategic response to the increasing complexity of technology stacks and the need for niche expertise. For instance, in the realm of application security, businesses may not require or cannot afford full-time, in-house security experts. Micro-outsourcing presents a solution by allowing companies to engage with specialist security teams who can conduct thorough security assessments, such as code reviews, on an as-needed basis. These teams scrutinize newly committed code to identify vulnerabilities, ensuring that security is tightly woven into the development lifecycle without necessitating a permanent increase in headcount.

This trend reflects a broader movement towards agility and cost-efficiency in software development. It enables organizations to tap into global talent pools for highly specialized tasks, such as AI optimization, UX testing, or GDPR compliance checks, without the long-term commitment of traditional outsourcing contracts. Micro-outsourcing also facilitates rapid scaling of capabilities to meet project demands, ensuring that the right skills are available at the right time.

Furthermore, micro-outsourcing aligns well with the Agile methodology, supporting iterative development and continuous integration/delivery models. By integrating external experts into specific stages of the development pipeline, companies can maintain a lean operational model while ensuring that their products benefit from best-in-class practices and knowledge.

In essence, micro-outsourcing enhances the adaptability of businesses in the fast-paced digital landscape, allowing them to remain competitive and innovative by leveraging specialized skills on-demand. This approach not only optimizes resource allocation but also fosters a collaborative ecosystem where external and internal teams work symbiotically to achieve common goals.

Understanding the Different Types of Outsourcing in Software Development

Outsourcing in software development is a multifaceted strategy, with each approach catering to specific business needs and scenarios. This book dedicates a section to dissect the various types of outsourcing, namely Domestic Outsourcing, Nearshoring, and Offshoring, each with its unique characteristics, advantages, and challenges.

Domestic outsourcing involves leveraging talent within the same country but in regions with a lower cost of living. For instance, in the U.S., there's a trend towards Appalachian Outsourcing or tapping into talent pools in states like Alabama and Mississippi. This approach offers substantial benefits, including cultural and linguistic alignment, currency uniformity, and often, minimal time zone differences. However, it comes with higher costs compared to offshoring. Also, there's a natural migration of tech talent towards coastal cities and tech hubs, which can limit the availability of skilled professionals in these lower-cost regions.

Nearshoring refers to outsourcing to neighboring countries, usually within a few hours' flight or in similar time zones. This model is exemplified by U.S. companies outsourcing to Costa Rica, or French companies partnering with Polish tech firms. The proximity offers advantages in communication and cultural similarity, which can significantly reduce the chances of misunderstandings and facilitate easier audits and compliance with data protection laws. However, nearshoring can be costlier than offshoring and may offer a more limited pool of technical talent and specialized expertise.

Offshoring is about partnering with vendors in geographically distant countries, primarily for cost advantages. This model opens doors to a vast talent pool and access to diverse technical expertise at significantly lower costs. For example, outsourcing to regions like India or Eastern

Europe provides access to highly skilled professionals at a fraction of the cost in Western countries. However, offshoring brings challenges like cultural differences, time zone disparities, and potential communication barriers.

Each outsourcing model comes with its set of pros and cons:

- Domestic Outsourcing: Ensures cultural and language compatibility and easier collaboration but comes at a higher cost and with potentially limited talent availability.

- Nearshoring: Offers smoother communication and cultural alignment, with easier management of intellectual property and legal compliance. It, however, still carries higher costs than offshoring and may present a limited talent pool.

- Offshoring: Provides significant cost savings and access to a vast pool of talent and unique expertise. The challenges lie in managing cultural differences, time zone variations, and ensuring effective communication.

Choosing the right outsourcing model requires careful consideration of your project's requirements, budget constraints, and strategic objectives. Whether it's leveraging the cost-effectiveness of offshoring, the cultural affinity of nearshoring, or the regional talent pools of domestic outsourcing, each model has its place in the global landscape of software development.

In this book, we explore these models in-depth, providing insights and real-world examples to help you make informed decisions that align with your business goals and project needs. By understanding the nuances of each outsourcing type, you can strategically navigate the global talent market and harness its full potential for your software development endeavors.

Exploring Outsourcing Models: Staff Augmentation vs. Project-Based Outsourcing

In the dynamic world of software development, companies often grapple with the decision of how to effectively manage their external workforce. Two prevalent models emerge in this scenario: Staff Augmentation and Project-Based Outsourcing. This section of the book delves into these models, elucidating their nuances, and weighing their pros and cons to guide you in making informed decisions.

Staff augmentation is a model where external professionals are seamlessly integrated into your existing team and processes. Under this model, you maintain full control over the project's trajectory, treating augmented staff as an extension of your in-house team. This approach allows for more direct oversight and a cohesive working environment, aligning external talent with your company's culture, methodologies, and goals.

Advantages of Staff Augmentation:

1. Enhanced Control: You retain direct oversight of the project, offering flexibility to steer it as per evolving requirements.
2. Cultural Alignment: Augmented staff blend into your company's culture, fostering a unified team ethos.
3. Adaptability: The model offers agility in adjusting team size and skill sets in response to project demands.
4. Continuity: It ensures continuity in internal processes and methodologies, providing a smoother workflow integration.

Disadvantages of Staff Augmentation:

1. Increased Management Overhead: Requires significant internal management effort and resources to supervise the augmented team.
2. Potential for Distraction: Internal resources may be stretched thin, potentially impacting core business functions.
3. Scaling Challenges: Rapid scaling up or down can be more cumbersome compared to project-based outsourcing.

Project-Based Outsourcing involves entrusting an entire project, or specific project components, to an external service provider. In this model, the outsourced team is responsible for managing and delivering the project, operating independently from your internal processes. This approach is often chosen for its cost-effectiveness and efficiency, especially for projects that require specialized skills or for managing workload peaks.

Advantages of Project-Based Outsourcing:

1. Cost-Efficiency: Typically more cost-effective, especially for large or specialized projects.
2. Expertise Access: Offers access to a wide range of specialized skills and technologies.
3. Focus on Core Business: Frees up internal resources, allowing your team to concentrate on core business activities.
4. Scalability: Easier to scale, as the outsourcing company manages resource allocation.

Disadvantages of Project-Based Outsourcing:

1. Reduced Control: Limited direct oversight can lead to concerns about the project aligning with company standards.
2. Integration Challenges: Potential difficulties in integrating the outsourced project with internal systems and processes.
3. Cultural and Communication Barriers: May encounter challenges in communication and cultural alignment, impacting project execution.

Choosing between staff augmentation and project-based outsourcing hinges on several factors, including your project's complexity, internal resource availability, management capacity, and strategic objectives. Staff augmentation is ideal if you seek to bolster your team's capabilities while maintaining control and integrating external talent into your internal culture. In contrast, project-based outsourcing is more suited for discrete projects where specialized skills are required, or when you need to offload work to focus on core business functions.

While project-based outsourcing certainly holds merit for certain organizations, particularly those that do not specialize in software development or do not view it as a strategic asset for long-term competitiveness, this book is focused on unraveling the intricacies of making staff augmentation a successful endeavor for your organization. Our aim is to delve into how staff augmentation can be strategically utilized to create enduring value for your company. We explore the nuances of integrating external talent seamlessly into your existing teams and processes, ensuring that this collaboration elevates your company's capabilities and drives long-term success. This book serves as a guide to harnessing the full potential of staff augmentation, transforming it into a powerful tool for sustained organizational growth and innovation.

When Not to Outsource

Understanding when not to outsource is as crucial as knowing when to do so, especially in scenarios where regulatory and legal considerations come into play. For instance, compliance with specific regulatory frameworks like FedRAMP poses a unique challenge. These frameworks often include stringent citizenship or residency requirements and dictate where and how the work can be executed, potentially restricting the feasibility of outsourcing to certain locations. It's imperative for businesses to meticulously analyze these requirements to ensure their outsourcing strategies are compliant.

Additionally, the protection of Intellectual Property (IP) is a paramount concern. The strength of IP laws and their enforcement varies globally, and in countries with weaker IP protections, outsourcing could jeopardize sensitive IP that gives a business its competitive edge. Conducting thorough due diligence on the IP landscape of the potential outsourcing location is essential to safeguard valuable IP.

Moreover, navigating the complex web of technology restrictions imposed by governments, like the U.S. Treasury Department, adds another layer of complexity. Working with entities in countries under sanctions or embargoes, such as Cuba, Iran, North Korea, Sudan, and Syria, can lead to legal complications and should be approached with caution. Ensuring compliance with international trade regulations is crucial before initiating any outsourcing arrangements in these regions.

 If software development is a core competency of your business and central to your competitive advantage, outsourcing may not be the best approach. Keeping this function in-house ensures direct control over the processes and outputs, fostering innovation and maintaining a strategic edge.

Lastly, data privacy regulations, epitomized by the European Union's General Data Protection Regulation (GDPR), impose stringent standards on data handling and transfer. These regulations can significantly limit the ability to outsource projects that involve the processing of protected data outside the jurisdiction of these laws. Collaborating closely with legal and compliance teams is vital to navigate these data privacy landscapes effectively and make informed decisions that align with both business goals and legal requirements.

In essence, while outsourcing offers numerous advantages, it's not without its challenges. Factors such as regulatory compliance, IP protection, government-imposed technology restrictions, and strict data privacy laws play a pivotal role in determining the feasibility and suitability of outsourcing for a particular project or operation. Businesses must carefully evaluate these factors to ensure that their outsourcing decisions are both strategically sound and legally compliant.

Tax Implications of Outsourcing

Back in 2017, the Trump administration passed the Tax Cuts & Jobs Act. Nested within this act was a financial time bomb for companies that innovate using software, which I believe is partially why we're seeing so many tech layoffs in the new year. The IRS guidance, Notice 2023-63, issued in September set us on the path we are on today, and without action by Congress, it will hamper US innovation for the foreseeable future and make it more expensive for product and engineering leaders around the country to satisfy their customers' needs.

Section 174 changes primarily involve the treatment of Research and Development (R&D) expenses. Under the new rules, companies can no longer immediately deduct these expenses. Instead, they must capitalize and amortize them over five years (for domestic expenses) and 15 years (for foreign expenses). This change, effective from 2022, impacts how businesses manage their R&D costs and may lead to reconsideration of investment strategies in innovation and development projects. The impact is particularly significant for technology and pharmaceutical sectors, where R&D is a major part of business operations.

The changes to Section 174 significantly impact companies that develop software. These companies, which typically invest heavily in R&D, are now required to capitalize and amortize their R&D expenses over several years rather than deducting them immediately. This affects their cash flow and could lead to a reconsideration of how much they invest in developing new software or updating existing ones. The change could also influence decisions on whether to pursue certain innovative projects, given the longer period for recovering these costs.

In a global context, many countries offer more favorable tax treatments for R&D activities compared to the updated U.S. Section 174. For instance, countries like Canada, the UK, and France provide tax credits or immediate deductions for R&D expenses, encouraging innovation and development. This contrast means U.S. companies might find themselves at a competitive disadvantage, especially in technology and pharmaceutical sectors. The change in the U.S. could potentially shift the dynamics of where companies choose to invest in R&D, with some considering relocation of these activities to countries with more beneficial tax regimes.

Let's compare this to Switzerland, a notoriously expensive place to do business, but a place where companies like Google have huge R&D facilities. Qualifying expenses can attract an additional tax deduction, with qualifying personnel expenses receiving a "lift-up" of 35% to cover other R&D costs, and third-party costs (contract R&D) being eligible based on 80% of invoiced costs.

These changes are costing companies real money, with Microsoft reporting $4.8B and Netflix $368M. Companies like Google were already amortizing their investments, so it didn't have a similar impact. This is traditionally how I managed my engineering budgets, amortizing over the "useful life" of 4-5 years, but with the change to code requiring offshored work to be amortized at 15 years it would have destroyed my last engineering budget.

These changes are already having a significant impact on startups. Here's how:

- Increased Cash Flow Challenges: The requirement to capitalize and amortize R&D expenses over several years, rather than deducting them immediately, could strain the limited cash reserves of startups. This change could impact their ability to invest in new projects or sustain ongoing ones.
- Reevaluation of R&D Strategies: Startups may need to reevaluate their R&D strategies, focusing on projects with the most significant potential impact or return on investment. This shift could lead to a more cautious approach to R&D spending.
- Difficulty in Attracting Investment: Investors often look for tax-efficient operations. The reduced immediate tax benefits from

R&D might make startups less attractive to potential investors, potentially impacting their ability to raise capital.

- Impact on Innovation and Growth: Since startups are key drivers of innovation, the changes could have a broader impact on the rate of technological advancement and market disruption. Startups might need to slow down or scale back their innovation efforts due to budget constraints.
- Consideration of Alternative Funding Sources: To offset the reduced tax benefits, startups might need to explore alternative funding sources, such as grants, venture capital, or strategic partnerships.
- Global Competitive Disadvantages: Compared to countries offering more favorable R&D tax treatments, U.S. startups might find themselves at a competitive disadvantage. This could influence decisions around where to locate R&D activities.
- Adapting to Longer Financial Horizons: Startups may need to plan for a longer horizon to realize the financial benefits of their R&D spending. This could require adjustments in their financial forecasting and business models.
- Navigating Complex Tax Compliance: The changes add complexity to tax compliance, which could be particularly challenging for startups that typically have limited resources for managing complex tax matters.

In early January 2024, the IRS issued a small reprieve for software where the findings are separately bargained for and acquired for limited purposes, but they will not help most companies.

Today, around 65% of businesses outsource some or part of their software development. Much of the time, this is to overseas teams across the world. Changing the amortization rules from being able to deduct engineering expenses immediately, or on a useful life timeline, to 15 years represents a tidal shift in these expenses.

Previously, if a company made $1M in revenue, and spent $700K with their offshore vendor, their taxable income would be $300K, ignoring all other expenses. With the new rules, if a company was in the exact same situation using offshore development resources, their taxable income would be $953K. This has serious and substantial impacts to the ability to invest in software development.

In the midst of the challenges posed by the recent changes to Section 174 of the U.S. Tax Code, there is a glimmer of hope for companies, particularly startups and technology firms, in the form of Research and Development (R&D) tax credits. While these credits can't fully compensate for the increased burden caused by the new requirement to capitalize and amortize R&D expenses, they can play a critical role in mitigating financial losses and sustaining innovation efforts.

R&D tax credits are incentives designed to encourage investment in innovation. They allow companies to reduce their tax liability by a certain percentage of their qualified R&D expenditures. Unlike deductions, which reduce taxable income, tax credits directly reduce the amount of tax owed, dollar-for-dollar.

In response to the changes in the U.S. tax code, specifically the amendments to Section 174, heads of engineering in U.S. companies should consider several strategic responses:

- Reassess R&D Budgets and Projects: With the requirement to capitalize and amortize R&D expenses over several years, immediate tax deductions for these expenses will no longer be available. This change necessitates a thorough review of R&D budgets and projects to prioritize those with the highest potential return on investment or strategic importance.
- Focus on Cost-Effective R&D Strategies: Engineering leaders should explore more cost-effective R&D strategies. This might involve adopting lean methodologies, optimizing resource allocation, or considering collaborative approaches such as partnerships or outsourcing to manage costs better.
- Explore Alternative Funding Sources: Given the reduced tax benefits for R&D, exploring alternative funding sources for

innovation projects, such as grants, venture capital, or strategic partnerships, becomes more important.

- Advocate for Favorable Policies: Participate in industry associations and policy discussions to advocate for more supportive R&D tax policies. This can include lobbying for changes that could benefit the industry and the innovation ecosystem as a whole.

- Stay Informed and Adapt: Keep abreast of ongoing tax policy developments and be prepared to adapt R&D strategies as necessary. This includes staying updated on any potential revisions to the tax code and being ready to modify financial planning and project prioritization accordingly.

- Enhance Cross-Functional Collaboration: Increasing collaboration with finance and accounting teams is crucial to understand the implications of the tax code changes on project costs and overall budgeting. Clear communication between departments will aid in aligning R&D activities with the company's financial strategies.

- Leverage Technology and Innovation: Investing in technology and innovative approaches can help optimize R&D processes, potentially reducing costs and increasing efficiency, thereby partially offsetting the impact of the tax changes.

- Employee Engagement and Communication: It's important to communicate with R&D teams about how these changes might impact their work. Keeping the team informed and engaged is crucial for maintaining morale and productivity.

- Global Strategy Consideration: Consider the global landscape of R&D incentives. Some companies may explore conducting R&D activities in countries with more favorable tax treatments, like Switzerland or certain EU countries, to leverage better incentives.

- Regular Review and Adjustment: Regularly review and adjust R&D strategies in response to both internal project outcomes and external regulatory changes. This dynamic approach will

help maintain agility and competitiveness in a changing fiscal
environment.

These strategies aim to navigate the altered fiscal landscape while
continuing to foster innovation and maintain a competitive edge in the
market.

In summary, Section 174 of the US Tax Cut & Jobs Act is going to make
software development in the US more expensive. It will likely result in
more tech layoffs, but may be balanced by pulling some jobs back into
the US. It will also result in companies deciding to purchase more SaaS
rather than develop solutions inhouse. Either way, it will make US
companies less competitive globally, startups less competitive, and
doing business more expensive, until Congress acts.

Traditional Advice on How to Succeed Outsourcing

The journey of outsourcing is riddled with complexities and pitfalls. Companies often concentrate on selecting countries, cities, and vendors, and negotiating costs, but overlook the critical step of evaluating which processes are suitable for outsourcing. This lack of a systematic approach leads to missteps like outsourcing core processes that should remain under the company's direct control, resulting in eventual repatriation of these processes.

Moreover, many companies fail to fully appreciate the risks associated with outsourcing. Simple cost-benefit analyses do not capture the whole picture. Once processes are transferred, vendors might gain leverage, posing a challenge to the organization's ability to swiftly reintegrate these processes if needed. This underestimation of risks often leaves companies vulnerable to vendor-imposed conditions like unexpected price hikes.

Another oversight is the narrow lens through which processes are evaluated. Companies often don't consider all available outsourcing options, such as local outsourcing, joint ventures, or establishing captive centers. This limited view can lead to choosing organizational forms that do not align with the company's needs. The focus is frequently only on direct costs, neglecting the impact of process interdependencies, which can significantly influence the cost-benefit analysis.

To navigate these turbulent waters successfully, companies must adopt a more nuanced and strategic approach to outsourcing. This involves a thorough evaluation of business processes, understanding the varying levels of operational and structural risks, and choosing the right organizational structure that aligns with these risks.

In essence, outsourcing is not merely a cost-cutting exercise but a strategic decision that requires careful deliberation and planning.

Companies that approach outsourcing with a holistic view, recognizing its potential to offer strategic advantages like product customization, development cycle acceleration, and profit margin enhancement, are likely to achieve greater success. The key is to start with a strategic vision and then tactically implement outsourcing, ensuring it aligns with the broader business objectives.

Agile Manifesto and Outsourcing

All too often we think the agile manifesto only applies to in-house employees. When we do this, we take away all of the raw power it has given us to transform the way we develop software.

The Agile Manifesto, established in February 2001 by seventeen software developers at the Snowbird ski resort in Utah, represents a significant shift in the software development paradigm. This manifesto was crafted to address the limitations and rigidness inherent in traditional, plan-heavy software development approaches. It introduces a new, more flexible methodology that emphasizes adaptability and responsiveness.

At its core, the Agile Manifesto prioritizes four key values: Firstly, it places individuals and interactions above processes and tools, underscoring the importance of direct communication and collaboration among team members and with clients. Secondly, it values working software over comprehensive documentation, focusing on delivering functional and effective software rather than extensive documentation. Thirdly, customer collaboration is emphasized over contract negotiation, encouraging ongoing engagement with the customer for feedback and adjustments throughout the development process. Lastly, the manifesto highlights the importance of responding to change over following a set plan, advocating for adaptability to changes in requirements and environment during the project lifecycle.

Alongside these values, the manifesto is further supported by twelve principles that guide the implementation of agile methodologies. These principles emphasize aspects such as adaptability, customer satisfaction, simplicity, regular reflection for self-improvement, maintaining a sustainable development pace, and the significance of face-to-face communication.

The introduction of the Agile Manifesto marked a transformative moment in the software industry, steering away from the conventional 'waterfall' approach towards a more iterative, flexible development process. This approach allows development teams to better adapt to changing needs and deliver value to customers more effectively, thereby revolutionizing the field of software development.

It goes as follows:

Manifesto for Agile Software Development

"We are uncovering better ways of developing

software by doing it and helping others do it.

Through this work we have come to value:

Individuals and interactions over processes and tools

Working software over comprehensive documentation

Customer collaboration over contract negotiation

Responding to change over following a plan.

That is, while there is value in the items on

the right, we value the items on the left more."

When companies decide to outsource their software development, they often unknowingly set aside the core principles of Agile that they may adhere to with their in-house teams. This deviation from Agile principles in outsourcing scenarios is not uncommon, but it significantly undermines the potential benefits of Agile methodologies.

A major factor in this shift is the perception of different dynamics in play when working with external teams. Companies often revert to more traditional, rigid forms of software management, primarily due to a combination of factors like time zone differences, language barriers, and most significantly, trust issues. For instance, the time zone differences can make it challenging to coordinate synchronous communication and collaboration, a key aspect of Agile. This leads to a reliance on documentation and less frequent updates, moving away from the Agile emphasis on regular interactions and iterative feedback.

Language barriers further compound these issues, making effective communication more challenging and potentially leading to misunderstandings or misinterpretations of requirements and feedback. This can result in a fallback to more documentation-heavy approaches as a perceived safeguard against communication gaps.

However, the most impactful factor is often the underlying trust issues between companies and their outsourced partners. There's a common apprehension about the quality of work and adherence to deadlines, which leads companies to impose stricter controls and oversight. Such an approach is contrary to Agile's principles of collaboration and empowerment. It tends to ignore the fact that Agile methodologies can be successfully applied in outsourced environments, just as they are in-house, by building a foundation of trust, clear communication, and mutual respect.

By reverting to traditional management styles with outsourced teams, companies miss out on the advantages Agile offers – such as flexibility, faster turnaround times, and a product more attuned to customer needs. This shift not only undermines the efficiency and effectiveness of the development process but can also lead to a disjointed approach where the internal and outsourced teams operate under fundamentally different methodologies. This inconsistency can further exacerbate challenges in integration, quality assurance, and overall project cohesion.

The concerns around outsourcing software development, such as the deviation from Agile principles, time zone challenges, language barriers, and trust issues, are indeed valid and prevalent in the industry. However, these obstacles should not deter organizations from realizing the full potential of Agile methodologies, even in an offshore setting. This book is designed to address precisely these challenges, offering a comprehensive framework that guides you in effectively leveraging the benefits of Agile with your outsourced teams.

Our framework acknowledges the complexities of working with outsourced teams and provides actionable strategies to navigate these intricacies. We emphasize the importance of establishing a robust communication system, aligned with Agile practices, that transcends geographical and linguistic barriers. By implementing the right tools and processes, and fostering a culture of openness and collaboration, you can ensure that your outsourced team is not just an external entity, but an integral part of your Agile ecosystem.

Moreover, we delve into building and maintaining trust, a critical aspect often overlooked in outsourced relationships. The book offers insights on creating a transparent environment where expectations are clearly defined, progress is openly tracked, and feedback is continuously exchanged. This approach not only strengthens the partnership but also aligns the outsourced team more closely with your company's Agile practices and goals.

We also provide guidance on practical aspects, such as aligning time zones for effective collaboration, overcoming language barriers through training and cultural exchange, and ensuring consistent application of Agile methodologies across all teams. By addressing these challenges head-on, we equip you with the knowledge to turn potential outsourcing pitfalls into opportunities for enhanced productivity and innovation.

In essence, this book is not just about managing outsourced teams; it's about integrating them seamlessly into your Agile journey. With the framework and strategies outlined here, you can ensure that your outsourced teams are not only adopting Agile practices but are also contributing significantly to your project's success. You'll learn to harness the full potential of your outsourced teams, making them a valuable asset in your Agile endeavors, and ultimately, achieving the most from these collaborations.

Levelsetting Agile Norms

In order to proceed, we need to first level set our agile norms. These are the expectations that all executives, and employee team members, and outsourced team members need to have in order for an Agile Outsourcing framework to work.

Continuous Delivery of Valuable Software

The concept of continuously delivering valuable software to customers is central to modern software development practices, especially in the context of Agile methodologies. This approach revolves around the idea of constantly providing users with functional, high-quality software that meets their evolving needs in a timely manner.

Continuously delivering valuable software necessitates a shift from traditional, long development cycles to a more dynamic and iterative process. This means breaking down the software project into smaller, manageable pieces, often referred to as iterations or sprints. Each of these iterations results in a potentially shippable product increment - a version of the software that includes new or improved features that deliver value to the customer.

This approach offers several advantages. Firstly, it allows for rapid response to changes in customer needs or market dynamics. Since the software development process is iterative, new requirements or changes can be incorporated into the next iteration, ensuring that the final product remains relevant and valuable.

Secondly, continuous delivery fosters closer collaboration between developers, stakeholders, and customers. Regular feedback loops are established, enabling immediate adjustments based on user feedback or changing business goals. This ongoing dialogue ensures that the software evolves in a direction that is aligned with the user's expectations and needs.

Moreover, this method reduces the risk associated with software development. By delivering software in small, frequent increments, issues can be identified and rectified early in the development process. This not only improves the quality of the software but also minimizes the cost and effort required to address problems later in the development cycle.

In the context of outsourcing, continuously delivering valuable software requires clear communication, robust project management, and a strong alignment of the outsourced team with the client's objectives. The outsourced team must be fully integrated into the development process, with a clear understanding of the project's goals, priorities, and user expectations.

Acceptance of Changing Requirements

Accepting changing requirements, even late in development, is a fundamental tenet of Agile methodologies and a significant competitive advantage in today's fast-paced and evolving market. This flexibility allows companies to adapt to new information, changing market conditions, or evolving customer needs, ensuring that the final product remains relevant and valuable.

In traditional software development models, requirements are often defined at the beginning of a project and remain largely fixed. This approach can lead to a final product that is disconnected from current user needs or market trends, especially in long-term projects. In contrast, Agile methodologies embrace the notion that change is inevitable and often beneficial. By accepting changes, even late in the development cycle, companies can pivot or adjust their strategies to align with new insights or demands, ensuring the product's relevance and market fit.

This adaptability is a powerful competitive edge. It allows businesses to respond quickly to competitors, capitalize on emerging opportunities, or address unforeseen challenges, keeping them ahead in the market. It also reflects a customer-centric approach to development, where feedback and user experience drive the evolution of the product.

However, managing changing requirements requires robust processes and effective communication, particularly in the context of outsourced development. Clear channels of communication between the client and the development team are essential, ensuring that changes are understood, evaluated, and implemented effectively. Agile practices like regular stand-ups, sprint planning meetings, and retrospectives are vital in this regard, as they facilitate ongoing dialogue and alignment.

Additionally, a flexible architecture and development practices that can accommodate changes without significant rework or disruption are crucial. This includes modular design, adherence to coding standards, and comprehensive testing procedures.

In outsourcing arrangements, it is essential to ensure that the partner is capable of and comfortable with Agile methodologies and the idea of iterative development. The contract and working relationship should allow for flexibility and changes, with clear mechanisms for discussing and approving these changes.

In summary, accepting changing requirements, even late in development, is not just about being adaptable; it's about staying relevant, responsive, and customer-focused. It allows companies to continuously refine and enhance their product, ensuring it meets the actual needs of its users. This approach requires a combination of Agile practices, effective communication, and a strong partnership between the client and the outsourcing team, but the payoff is a product that is more likely to succeed in the market.

Delivering Frequent Working Software

Delivering working software frequently, rather than adhering to prolonged development cycles, is a cornerstone of Agile methodologies and a critical practice in modern software development. This approach emphasizes the value of delivering small, incremental pieces of software regularly – it could be monthly, bi-weekly, weekly, or even daily. This shift from traditional, often annual or semi-annual, releases to more frequent updates is transformative, offering numerous benefits to both the development team and the client.

In traditional software development models, long intervals between releases often lead to accumulating changes that can be challenging to manage and integrate. This approach can also delay feedback, making it harder to adjust course based on user reactions or market trends. Frequent delivery addresses these challenges head-on. By breaking down the development process into smaller segments, teams can focus on delivering specific functionalities or improvements in a manageable timeframe. This makes it easier to ensure quality, as each increment undergoes testing and review before being released.

For clients, this means receiving functional software at regular intervals, providing opportunities to review progress, offer feedback, and see tangible results more quickly. This ongoing delivery cycle fosters a collaborative environment where the client is actively involved in the development process, helping to guide the product's direction based on real-world use and feedback.

In the context of outsourced development, frequent delivery helps maintain transparency and trust. Regular updates offer clients a clear view of the project's progress and the quality of work being produced. It also enables better risk management, as issues can be identified and addressed early in the development process, rather than after a lengthy and costly development phase.

Implementing this approach requires a well-structured workflow and effective project management. Agile practices like Scrum or Kanban, with their emphasis on iterative development and regular sprint reviews, are well-suited to support frequent software delivery. It's also important for the development team, whether in-house or outsourced, to have a robust understanding of Agile principles and the discipline to adhere to the defined development and delivery cadences.

The technological infrastructure plays a significant role as well. Continuous Integration and Continuous Deployment (CI/CD) pipelines facilitate the rapid and reliable delivery of software by automating the build, test, and deployment processes. This automation is crucial for maintaining the pace and quality of frequent releases.

In summary, delivering working software frequently is about more than just speed; it's about responsiveness, quality, and collaboration. It enables teams to respond quickly to changes, ensures ongoing alignment with user needs, and fosters a culture of continuous improvement and customer focus. For companies embracing outsourcing, it's vital to partner with firms that understand and practice these principles, ensuring that the outsourced development aligns with these agile tenets.

Business and Developers Working Together

The principle that business people and developers must collaborate closely throughout a project is pivotal in Agile methodology, and it holds significant implications for teams working with outsourced software development. This collaboration is rooted in the belief that the best outcomes are achieved when there is a seamless flow of communication and a shared understanding between those who understand the business requirements (business people) and those who translate these needs into software solutions (developers).

In the context of outsourcing, adhering to this principle requires an intentional effort to integrate external development teams into the company's internal processes. This integration involves more than just regular meetings or status updates; it necessitates a deeper level of collaboration where outsourced teams are given access to internal resources and are not isolated or 'walled off' from the core team.

Ensuring daily interaction between business teams and outsourced developers is crucial for several reasons. First, it fosters a shared understanding of project goals, priorities, and challenges. Developers gain a clearer insight into the business context and objectives, enabling them to make more informed decisions and propose solutions that align closely with the business's needs. Conversely, business stakeholders gain a better appreciation of the technical aspects of the project, which can inform more realistic expectations and decision-making.

To facilitate this level of collaboration, companies can employ various strategies. One effective approach is the use of collaborative tools and platforms that support real-time communication, project tracking, and document sharing. These tools help bridge the physical gap between in-house teams and outsourced partners, ensuring that everyone is on the same page, regardless of their location.

Another key aspect is establishing a cultural match between the in-house and outsourced teams. This involves aligning work ethics, communication styles, and project management methodologies. It's essential for both sides to understand and respect each other's work culture to foster a harmonious working relationship.

It's also vital to involve outsourced teams in key meetings and decision-making processes, treating them as an extension of the in-house team rather than as external contractors. This could include participation in daily stand-ups, planning meetings, review sessions, and retrospectives. Such involvement ensures that outsourced developers are not just coding to specification but are actively engaged in shaping the product's direction.

In summary, close collaboration between business people and developers is not just a recommendation in Agile methodology; it's a necessity for the success of any project, especially in an outsourcing arrangement. By fostering daily interaction and integration between internal teams and outsourced partners, companies can achieve more cohesive, efficient, and effective software development processes. This collaborative approach leads to a more transparent, responsive, and ultimately successful project outcome.

Creating Healthy Ecosystems

Creating a healthy ecosystem in software development, particularly in the context of outsourcing, is central to achieving project success. This involves building projects around motivated individuals, providing them with the necessary environment and support, and trusting them to accomplish the task at hand.

When working with outsourced teams, recognizing and fostering individual motivation is key. Motivated developers are more likely to be proactive, innovative, and committed to delivering high-quality work. Companies can nurture this motivation by understanding the personal and professional goals of their outsourced team members and aligning these goals with the project's objectives. This alignment helps create a sense of ownership and investment in the project's success.

Providing the right environment is equally crucial. This encompasses not just the physical workspace for in-house teams, but also the virtual environment for remote outsourced teams. Ensuring that outsourced teams have access to the necessary tools, technologies, and resources is essential. This could mean providing access to collaborative software, project management tools, or even ensuring they have a stable and robust internet connection. Additionally, creating an inclusive and welcoming atmosphere, where outsourced team members feel valued and part of the larger team, plays a significant role in boosting morale and productivity.

Support is another pillar of this ecosystem. It involves offering guidance, mentorship, and constructive feedback. It's about creating a support system where outsourced team members can easily reach out for help or clarification without hesitation. Regular check-ins, open communication channels, and a supportive leadership approach are integral to this.

However, providing an environment and support is not enough unless there is also trust. Trusting the team to get the job done is a fundamental Agile principle. This means resisting the urge to micromanage and instead, focusing on setting clear goals and expectations, and then allowing the team the autonomy to achieve these goals in their way. Trusting the team also means being open to their suggestions and ideas, and giving them the freedom to experiment and take calculated risks.

It's important to remember that trust goes both ways. Just as the company needs to trust its outsourced team, the team must also feel that they can trust the company to be fair, transparent, and supportive. This mutual trust is the cornerstone of a healthy working relationship and is critical for the success of any outsourced project.

In conclusion, building a healthy ecosystem in an outsourced software development project involves a holistic approach that focuses on motivation, environment, support, and trust. By fostering these elements, companies can create a productive and positive working relationship with their outsourced teams, leading to successful project outcomes and long-term partnerships.

Face to Face?

The Agile Manifesto emphasizes the importance of face-to-face conversation as the most efficient and effective method of conveying information within a development team. This principle, while straightforward in a co-located environment, presents unique challenges and opportunities in the context of outsourced software development.

In an outsourced setup, the geographical distance between the business leadership and the development team can create communication barriers. However, overcoming these barriers is not insurmountable; it requires commitment and creative approaches. One effective strategy is for engineering leadership and product management to physically visit the development centers. These visits are invaluable for relationship-building. By spending days or even weeks on-site, leadership can engage in direct, face-to-face interactions with the team. These interactions are not limited to work-related discussions; they extend to social activities, such as shared meals and team-building exercises. Such engagements foster trust, mutual respect, and a deeper understanding of the cultural and working dynamics of the outsourced team.

When on-site visits are not feasible, technology bridges the gap. Tools like Zoom or Microsoft Teams become essential, not just for their functionality, but for their ability to facilitate face-to-face communication virtually. Insisting on having cameras turned on during these virtual meetings is more than a procedural formality; it allows for the observation of non-verbal cues and body language, which are crucial components of effective communication. These subtle cues often convey more than words alone and can lead to a more nuanced understanding of team dynamics and individual sentiments.

Additionally, frequency of communication is key in outsourced environments. Daily interactions, whether for project updates, brainstorming sessions, or informal check-ins, help maintain a steady flow of information and keep everyone aligned. Regular communication not only ensures that everyone is on the same page but also builds a rhythm and routine that fosters a sense of teamwork and collaboration, despite the physical distance.

In summary, while face-to-face conversation in an outsourced environment requires more effort and planning, its benefits are significant. Physical visits, coupled with the judicious use of video conferencing tools and frequent communication, can effectively replicate the advantages of in-person interactions. This approach helps in building strong, collaborative relationships and ensures that the outsourced development team is well-integrated with the company's vision and goals.

Measuring Progress

In Agile software development, the primary metric for success is the delivery of working software. This principle underscores the fundamental goal of any software development effort – to create software that not only functions as intended but is also actively used and valued by its intended users. In the context of outsourcing, this becomes even more crucial to monitor and enforce.

In many traditional software development environments, metrics such as the number of tickets closed, Product Requirement Documents (PRDs) processed, or bugs fixed are often used as indicators of progress. While these metrics can provide insights into the workflow and efficiency of the development process, they can be misleading if not aligned with the ultimate goal of delivering usable software to customers. The risk in an outsourced environment is that these metrics might become the primary focus, overshadowing the real objective of delivering functional software.

For software to truly deliver value, it must not remain dormant in source control or be confined to a development environment. It needs to be integrated, tested, and deployed into a production environment where it can be accessed and used by customers. This is the final and most crucial step in the development process, as it is the point where the software starts to fulfill its intended purpose – solving real-world problems for its users.

To ensure that this principle is upheld in outsourced software development, it's important to establish clear communication and alignment on goals between the outsourcing partner and the client. Regular reviews and demonstrations of working software should be an integral part of the development cycle. These reviews provide an opportunity to validate the functionality, gather feedback, and make necessary adjustments. It also ensures that everyone, including stakeholders and development teams, remains focused on the end goal – delivering software that not only works but is also actively used and appreciated by its customers.

In conclusion, while traditional metrics of development progress are important, they should not overshadow the primary measure of success in Agile software development: the delivery of working software. For companies engaged in outsourcing, it is crucial to maintain a laser focus on this goal, ensuring that every effort contributes directly to creating software that meets customer needs and enhances their experience.

Sustainable Development

Sustainable development is a fundamental tenet of Agile processes, emphasizing the importance of maintaining a steady, manageable pace in software development. This concept is critical not just for the well-being of the team but also for the long-term success of the project. It applies equally to teams working in-house and those involved in outsourcing.

In the realm of Agile software development, sustainable development implies that all parties involved – sponsors, developers, and users – should be capable of sustaining a consistent work rhythm over an indefinite period. This balance is crucial. It means that while teams are expected to work efficiently and continuously improve their productivity, they should do so without overexerting themselves. The relentless push to work excessively long hours or to "burn the midnight oil" can be counterproductive, leading to burnout, retention issues, and a decline in the quality and security of the software produced.

For outsourced development teams, sustainable development ensures that the quality of work doesn't diminish over time due to fatigue or burnout. Teams that are overworked may initially show high productivity, but this is often not sustainable in the long run. Over time, it can lead to increased errors, lower morale, and higher turnover rates – all of which are detrimental to the overall success of the project.

Maintaining a sustainable pace also involves continuous learning and improvement. As teams become more experienced and familiar with the project, they should become more efficient. However, this increase in efficiency should not be misconstrued as an opportunity to exponentially increase workload. Instead, it should be viewed as a means to enhance the quality of work, foster innovation, and deliver greater value to the users.

In conclusion, sustainable development within Agile processes is about finding and maintaining the right balance. It's about ensuring that teams are productive and efficient, yet not overburdened. This balance is key to fostering a healthy work environment, retaining talent, and consistently delivering high-quality software that meets users' needs. For companies outsourcing their software development, it is essential to ensure that their partners also adhere to this principle, creating a mutually beneficial working relationship centered on long-term success and sustainability.

Attention to Technical Excellence

Focusing on technical excellence is a core aspect of Agile methodology, emphasizing the significance of quality and thoughtful design in enhancing agility and overall project success. This approach is particularly crucial in the context of software development outsourcing, where maintaining high standards can be challenging due to varied processes and priorities across different teams.

Technical excellence in Agile processes implies a commitment to making long-term architectural decisions that prioritize sustainability and effectiveness over short-term gains. It involves adopting strategies that foresee future needs and changes, thus avoiding the pitfalls of quick fixes that may lead to technical debt. Such an approach ensures that the software architecture is robust, scalable, and adaptable to evolving requirements.

Another essential component of technical excellence is the consistent practice of writing automated tests. This practice ensures that each piece of code is thoroughly tested, reducing bugs and improving overall code quality. It also streamlines the development process, as automated tests provide quick feedback on new changes, making it easier to identify and fix issues early in the development cycle.

Improving the codebase every time it is touched is another aspect of this principle. This approach, often referred to as code refactoring, involves restructuring existing code without changing its external behavior to improve its internal structure. It's about leaving the code better than you found it, which ultimately leads to a more maintainable and efficient codebase.

Management plays a pivotal role in fostering an environment that values technical excellence. It's crucial for leadership to understand that the pressures of business needs should not overshadow the importance of quality and sound technical practices. Encouraging an environment where technical excellence is a priority means providing the necessary time and resources for teams to focus on quality, offering training and tools needed for best practices, and recognizing and rewarding efforts towards improving code quality and design.

For outsourced development teams, it's vital to ensure that they share this commitment to technical excellence. This can be achieved through clear communication of expectations, regular reviews of code and architecture, and collaborative efforts in decision-making processes regarding technical approaches. By focusing on technical excellence, companies can ensure that their software products are not just functional but also robust, adaptable, and capable of meeting the dynamic demands of the business landscape.

Simplicity

In the realm of agile software development, particularly in the context of outsourcing, the principle of simplicity holds a pivotal place. Embracing simplicity means striving for the most straightforward and efficient approach to solving problems, a concept often encapsulated in the phrase "maximizing the amount of work not done." This idea, though seemingly counterintuitive, underscores the importance of focusing on essential functionalities and avoiding unnecessary complexity in software design and development.

Applying this principle to outsourced projects requires careful consideration. For instance, when dealing with outsourced teams, it becomes crucial to articulate requirements clearly and concisely, avoiding the temptation to over-engineer solutions. The goal is to deliver software that meets the core needs of the users without getting bogged down in features that don't add significant value.

In practice, this means prioritizing tasks and focusing on what's truly important for the project's success. For the client, it involves resisting the urge to request additional features that do not align with the primary objectives. For the development team, it means applying their expertise to identify and implement the most straightforward solutions that meet these objectives. This approach not only saves time and resources but also ensures that the final product is user-friendly and not overburdened with superfluous elements.

Furthermore, simplicity in agile development fosters better collaboration between clients and outsourced teams. Clear, straightforward objectives make it easier for remote teams to understand the client's vision and work efficiently towards achieving it. In an outsourced setting, where direct, face-to-face interactions are limited, the value of simplicity cannot be overstated.

Therefore, in outsourcing, as in all agile environments, simplicity is not just a design principle but a strategic approach that guides every aspect of the development process. It is about doing less but achieving more, focusing on quality over quantity, and ensuring that every effort is directed towards delivering real, tangible value to the end user.

Self-Organizing Teams

In the context of Agile development, the concept of self-organizing teams represents a fundamental shift from traditional hierarchical project management structures. It's a principle that empowers team members to take ownership of their work, make decisions, and solve problems collaboratively without being micromanaged. However, this concept is often misunderstood, leading to misconceptions about what self-organization entails and what it doesn't.

Self-organizing doesn't mean a lack of structure or leadership. Contrary to some beliefs, it doesn't imply that teams operate in a free-for-all environment. There's still a need for leadership, but it's more about facilitation and guidance rather than command and control. Leaders in a self-organizing environment set the vision, provide context, and ensure that the team has the resources and environment they need to succeed.

A common misconception is that self-organizing teams don't need any form of management or oversight. In reality, these teams work within the boundaries and goals set by the organization. They have the autonomy to decide how to achieve these goals but are not working in isolation from the rest of the organization.

Best practices for self-organizing teams, especially in an outsourced environment, include:

1. Clear Communication: Establishing clear communication channels and regular check-ins is vital. This ensures that everyone is aligned with the project goals and understands their roles and responsibilities.
2. Defined Goals and Boundaries: Teams need a clear understanding of what they are expected to achieve and the constraints within which they must operate. This clarity helps in prioritizing tasks and making informed decisions.
3. Trust and Empowerment: One of the keys to successful self-organization is trust. Management must trust that the team has

the skills and judgment to make good decisions. In turn, teams must be empowered to take those decisions without fearing negative repercussions for every mistake.

4. Continuous Learning and Adaptation: Self-organizing teams should continually reflect on their performance and seek ways to improve. This might involve adapting processes, trying new tools, or acquiring new skills.

5. Collaboration and Respect: Effective self-organization requires a high level of collaboration and mutual respect among team members. Each member's opinion is valued, and decisions are often made collectively.

In outsourcing, implementing self-organization can be challenging due to cultural differences, time zone discrepancies, and communication barriers. However, with the right approach, these challenges can be overcome. Outsourced teams can be integrated into the Agile process by clearly defining the scope of their autonomy, establishing regular communication routines, and building a culture of trust and collaboration.

In summary, self-organizing teams in Agile are about empowering team members to take control of their work within the framework of the organization's objectives. It's not an abandonment of leadership but a redefinition of it, focusing on enabling teams to perform at their best through trust, clarity, and support.

Frequent Retrospection

Frequent retrospectives are a pivotal practice in Agile development, serving as a cornerstone for continuous improvement and team effectiveness. These retrospectives are dedicated sessions where teams reflect on their recent work, discuss what went well, identify areas for improvement, and plan actionable steps to enhance their future performance. The cadence of these retrospectives is typically at the end of each sprint or iteration, allowing for timely and relevant feedback.

The necessity of frequent retrospectives cannot be overstated. They provide a structured opportunity for team members to voice their opinions, concerns, and suggestions in a safe and constructive environment. This practice fosters a culture of openness and trust, which is essential for the healthy functioning of any team, especially in an outsourced or distributed team setup.

In practice, retrospectives manifest as structured meetings with a clear agenda. They typically start with a review of the goals set in the previous retrospective, followed by a discussion on what went well, what didn't go as planned, and what could be improved. It's crucial to focus on processes and behaviors rather than individuals to maintain a positive and constructive atmosphere. The facilitator, often a Scrum Master or team lead, plays a key role in guiding the discussion, ensuring that every team member has a chance to contribute, and keeping the conversation productive.

One of the critical aspects of retrospectives is the actionability of the outcomes. It's not just about discussing issues; it's about committing to specific changes or experiments to try in the next iteration. This action-oriented approach ensures that retrospectives lead to tangible improvements rather than becoming mere discussion forums.

Teams also need mechanisms to hold themselves accountable for the actions they agree upon in retrospectives. This could involve setting clear owners for each action item, incorporating them into the team's workflow, and reviewing the progress of these action items in subsequent retrospectives. Accountability ensures that the team not only identifies areas for improvement but also actively works towards addressing them.

In the context of outsourced teams, retrospectives are even more critical. They help bridge the gap caused by physical distance, cultural differences, and varied working styles. In such settings, it's essential to use technology effectively to facilitate these meetings and ensure everyone has an equal opportunity to participate. Tools like video conferencing, collaborative digital whiteboards, and retrospective-specific software can be invaluable.

In conclusion, frequent retrospectives are a vital mechanism for Agile teams to reflect, learn, and continuously improve. They foster a culture of transparency and continuous learning, which is crucial for the success of any project. For outsourced teams, retrospectives are not just a tool for process improvement but also a means to strengthen team cohesion and alignment despite the challenges of geographical dispersion.

Updated Agile Manifesto for Agile Outsourcing

In the evolving landscape of software development, the integration of outsourced teams presents both opportunities and challenges. Recognizing this, we introduce a novel paradigm in this book: Agile Outsourcing. This approach not only retains the core principles of traditional Agile methodologies but also enriches them with the diverse perspectives that a globally distributed team brings. The new Agile Outsourcing model we propose is grounded in the belief that leveraging our varied locations, cultures, and backgrounds can significantly enhance customer value, elevate the quality of software, and foster the development of our team members.

Manifesto for Outsourced Agile Software Development

"We are uncovering better ways of developing

software by doing it and helping others do it.

Through this work we have come to value:

Individuals and interactions over processes and tools

Working software over comprehensive documentation

Customer collaboration over contract negotiation

Responding to change over following a plan.

We leverage our location, culture, and backgrounds

to increase customer value

increase the value of our software

and increase the quality of our fellow developers

That is, while there is value in the items on

the right, we value the items on the left more."

The essence of Agile Outsourcing lies in its ability to blend the agility and responsiveness of Agile methodologies with the breadth and depth of skills offered by outsourced teams. This fusion allows us to harness a broader spectrum of ideas, approaches, and techniques, contributing to richer, more innovative software solutions.

This section of the book is dedicated to introducing and exploring the new principles of Agile Outsourcing. Each chapter will delve into how these principles modify and expand upon traditional Agile norms, reflecting the realities and advantages of a distributed, multicultural development environment. We will examine how each principle adapts to the unique dynamics of outsourced collaboration, ensuring that the core Agile values of collaboration, customer focus, and continuous improvement are not only preserved but also enhanced in an outsourced setting.

Through this exploration, we aim to provide you with a comprehensive understanding of how Agile Outsourcing can revolutionize your approach to software development. By embracing these updated principles, you can unlock the full potential of your global teams, driving innovation, efficiency, and excellence in your software development endeavors.

Emphasize Global Collaboration Over Location Constraints

Original: "Individuals and interactions over processes and tools."

Updated: "Global collaboration and interactions over location constraints."

In the realm of Agile Outsourcing, we adapt the original Agile principle of prioritizing "individuals and interactions over processes and tools" to a more global context. The updated principle, "Global collaboration and interactions over location constraints," underscores the significance of seamless collaboration in a distributed team environment, transcending the traditional boundaries set by geographical locations.

This principle recognizes that in today's interconnected world, the physical location of team members is less important than their ability to collaborate effectively. The advent of advanced communication technologies and collaborative tools has made it possible for teams spread across the globe to work together as if they were in the same room. Emphasizing global collaboration means tapping into the diverse pool of talent and perspectives that a geographically dispersed team offers, which can lead to more innovative solutions and a broader understanding of global market needs.

However, this principle also acknowledges the challenges that come with outsourcing, such as differing time zones, cultural nuances, and communication styles. Addressing these challenges requires a deliberate focus on fostering strong, clear, and continuous communication channels. It involves creating an environment where team members feel connected and engaged, despite physical distances.

Moreover, this principle advocates for flexible interactions that respect the unique contexts of each team member, adapting processes and tools to suit different working conditions and cultural backgrounds. It's about creating a cohesive team culture that bridges the gap between various locations, ensuring that every team member feels equally valued and heard.

In practice, this means regular and structured virtual meetings, efficient use of collaborative software, and fostering a culture of open communication. It also involves adapting working hours where possible to maximize overlapping time zones for synchronous collaboration and ensuring that all team members have equal access to information and resources.

By adapting the principle of "individuals and interactions" to "global collaboration and interactions," Agile Outsourcing allows teams to leverage the strengths of their diverse backgrounds while overcoming the limitations imposed by geographical distances. This approach not only enhances team dynamics but also drives innovation and efficiency in software development projects.

Enhance Flexibility for Changing Requirements Across Time Zones

Original: "Welcome changing requirements, even late in development."

Updated: "Embrace changing requirements with flexible time zone management."

In adapting Agile principles to outsourced outsourcing, a significant enhancement is the shift from simply welcoming changing requirements to embracing these changes with flexible time zone management. This evolution acknowledges the unique challenges and opportunities presented by distributed teams working across various time zones.

In this updated paradigm, "Embrace changing requirements with flexible time zone management," processes are restructured to facilitate seamless collaboration across time zones. This approach calls for the implementation of methodologies that support asynchronous communication, ensuring that project documentation and updates are readily accessible and comprehensible for all team members, regardless of their geographical location. This documentation becomes a crucial tool, bridging the gap between different time zones and allowing for continuous progress without the need for real-time interaction.

Moreover, this principle emphasizes the importance of avoiding regional silos within the software development process. It advocates for a structure where multiple teams, spread across different time zones, have the capability and the authority to work on any part of the application. This approach not only fosters a more cohesive and integrated development process but also enhances the collective ownership and quality of the final product.

Furthermore, the principle encourages product teams to engage with customers in various time zones. This global perspective is invaluable, as it brings diverse insights and feedback, ensuring that the product resonates with a wider audience and meets the needs of a global customer base.

To implement this principle effectively, companies must invest in robust communication tools and develop clear guidelines for asynchronous collaboration. They must also foster a culture of flexibility and responsiveness, where team members are trained and encouraged to adapt to changes swiftly, regardless of time zone constraints. By doing so, companies can leverage the full potential of their global talent pool, ensuring that their offshore outsourcing endeavors are agile, efficient, and aligned with their strategic objectives.

Prioritize Continuous Delivery with Cross-Regional Teams

Original: "Deliver working software frequently."

Updated: "Continuously deliver working software across regions."

The update to the Agile principle, "Deliver working software frequently," to "Continuously deliver working software across regions," marks a significant shift in the approach to software development in an outsourced, global context. This updated principle underscores the necessity of consistent and frequent software delivery, not just within a single team or location, but across multiple regional teams involved in the project.

In this globalized approach, the emphasis is on establishing a harmonious rhythm of software delivery that transcends geographical boundaries. The principle encourages the integration of cross-regional teams into the development cycle, ensuring that software updates and new features are rolled out in a coordinated manner across different time zones and locations. This method guarantees a steady stream of deliverables, maintaining the momentum of the project and ensuring that client needs are met promptly, irrespective of the teams' locations.

To implement this principle effectively, organizations must adopt a robust framework that facilitates synchronized workflows and communication across different regions. This could involve setting up overlapping working hours for teams in different time zones, ensuring there is a window each day for real-time collaboration and problem-solving. It also requires a strong emphasis on clear documentation and communication channels that keep all team members, regardless of location, on the same page regarding project status and upcoming deliverables.

Moreover, this principle necessitates the use of sophisticated project management tools and platforms that support real-time tracking and collaboration. These tools become the nexus of project coordination, allowing teams across the globe to update their progress, flag issues, and stay aligned with the overall project timeline and objectives.

The essence of this updated principle is to foster a truly global collaborative environment where continuous software delivery is not hindered by regional barriers. By doing so, organizations can leverage the diverse expertise and perspectives of their global workforce, resulting in software products that are not only delivered efficiently but also resonate with a global user base. This approach not only aligns with the Agile ethos of rapid and continuous delivery but also adapts it to the realities and opportunities of a globally distributed software development landscape.

Promote Daily Cooperation Across Borders

Original: "Business people and developers must work together daily."

Updated: "Business and development teams, regardless of location, must collaborate closely."

The updated Agile principle, "Business and development teams, regardless of location, must collaborate closely," expands the original principle of daily cooperation between business people and developers to a more inclusive, global perspective. This modification recognizes the growing trend of outsourcing in software development and emphasizes the importance of maintaining seamless collaboration across borders and time zones.

In the context of outsourcing, where development teams are often spread across various geographical locations, traditional face-to-face interactions are not always feasible. The revised principle calls for innovative approaches to collaboration that transcend physical boundaries. This includes leveraging digital communication platforms and tools that facilitate effective and regular interactions between business teams and developers, regardless of their physical locations. The aim is to ensure that the vision, goals, and progress of the project are transparent and aligned among all parties involved.

Key to this principle is the acknowledgment that frequent, clear, and open communication is vital for the success of outsourced projects. It means scheduling regular meetings, using video conferencing tools for more personal interaction, and establishing channels for continuous communication that accommodate different time zones. This approach helps bridge the gap between different cultures and working styles, fostering a shared understanding and a unified approach to project objectives.

Moreover, this principle highlights the necessity of adapting traditional Agile methodologies to suit the dynamics of a distributed team. It involves rethinking the ways in which business requirements are communicated and how feedback is gathered and implemented. The focus is on creating an inclusive environment where every team member, regardless of their location, feels valued and is able to contribute effectively to the project.

The essence of this updated principle is to encourage a culture of collaboration that transcends geographical barriers, ensuring that outsourced teams are as integrated and aligned with the business objectives as any in-house team would be. This principle not only promotes efficiency and productivity in a global setup but also helps in building a cohesive and synergized team dynamic, crucial for the success of any software development project.

Support and Trust in Distributed Teams

Original: "Build projects around motivated individuals. Give them the environment and support they need, and trust them to get the job done."

Updated: "Foster an environment of support and trust for distributed teams, empowering them to deliver effectively."

The updated Agile principle, "Foster an environment of support and trust for distributed teams, empowering them to deliver effectively," builds upon the original concept of creating a supportive environment for motivated individuals. This new iteration recognizes the unique challenges and dynamics of distributed teams, particularly in the context of outsourcing.

In an outsourced setting, where teams are often geographically dispersed, fostering a supportive and trusting environment becomes crucial. This principle underscores the importance of recognizing and adapting to the diverse needs of team members who are working in different locations, time zones, and cultural contexts. It involves creating a work culture where remote team members feel equally valued, heard, and involved as those who may be onsite.

Key aspects of this principle include establishing clear lines of communication, setting realistic expectations, and providing the necessary tools and resources for distributed teams to collaborate effectively. This might mean investing in better project management and communication tools, ensuring all team members have access to the same information, and adapting workflows to suit different time zones.

Trust plays a pivotal role in this principle. It's about entrusting distributed teams with responsibilities and believing in their capability to deliver without micromanagement. This trust is built through transparency, regular updates, and open channels for feedback and discussion. It also means respecting their autonomy and acknowledging the diverse expertise and perspectives they bring to the table.

Supporting distributed teams also involves recognizing and addressing the unique challenges they face, such as isolation or difficulties in accessing immediate support or guidance. Regular check-ins, team-building activities, and opportunities for professional growth can help mitigate these challenges and foster a sense of belonging and commitment.

Ultimately, this updated principle is about creating an inclusive and empowering environment that acknowledges the complexities of distributed teams while leveraging their potential to contribute effectively to the project's success. By fostering a culture of support and trust, organizations can harness the full potential of their outsourced talent, leading to higher productivity, better quality of work, and more successful project outcomes.

Utilize Diverse Communication Channels for Effective Conveyance

Original: "The most efficient and effective method of conveying information to and within a development team is face-to-face conversation."

Updated: "Efficient and effective communication, utilizing diverse channels, is essential in a globally distributed team."

The updated Agile principle, "Efficient and effective communication, utilizing diverse channels, is essential in a globally distributed team," recognizes the complexities of communication in the modern, globally distributed workspace. This principle is an evolution from the original focus on face-to-face conversation, acknowledging that while direct interaction remains invaluable, the reality of outsourced and remote teams necessitates a broader range of communication methods.

In the realm of outsourcing, where teams are often spread across different countries and time zones, relying solely on face-to-face interactions is impractical. However, this doesn't diminish the importance of personal, direct communication. Visits to different team locations play a crucial role in building trust, understanding cultural nuances, and forming stronger team bonds. Activities like shared meals, team-building exercises, or casual outings like karaoke or ping pong can significantly enhance team cohesion and understanding. These interactions provide invaluable context and depth to working relationships, fostering a more integrated and empathetic team environment.

Simultaneously, this principle emphasizes the importance of utilizing various communication tools and channels to maintain constant and effective dialogue. Tools like video conferencing, collaborative software, instant messaging, and project management platforms enable real-time collaboration and ensure that information is shared promptly and transparently. These tools help in bridging the gap caused by physical distance, making remote collaboration more seamless and inclusive.

Effective communication in a distributed team also involves adapting to the diverse communication styles and preferences of team members. This might include scheduling meetings at times that are convenient for multiple time zones, providing written summaries of discussions for those who couldn't attend in real time, or using asynchronous communication methods like email or shared documents for non-urgent matters.

Moreover, it's crucial to establish clear communication protocols and guidelines. These should outline the preferred channels for different types of communication, the expected response times, and best practices for ensuring clarity and reducing misunderstandings. Regular training and updates on effective communication tools and techniques can also be beneficial.

In essence, this updated principle recognizes that while face-to-face interaction remains a gold standard for effective communication, the realities of global teams require a multifaceted approach. By embracing diverse communication channels and still valuing personal interaction, businesses can ensure that their distributed teams operate cohesively, efficiently, and effectively.

Sustainable Development at a Global Scale

Original: "Agile processes promote sustainable development."

Updated: "Sustainable development practices should be maintained globally, accommodating different time zones and work cultures."

The updated Agile principle, "Sustainable development practices should be maintained globally, accommodating different time zones and work cultures," addresses the challenges of sustaining a consistent and effective work rhythm in a global outsourcing context. This principle expands on the original agile tenet of promoting sustainable development by acknowledging the complexities that arise when teams are dispersed across various time zones and cultural landscapes.

In a global outsourcing scenario, sustainable development goes beyond merely managing the workload and avoiding burnout. It involves harmonizing work practices and expectations across diverse geographical regions and cultural backgrounds. This harmonization requires an understanding and respect for different working hours, public holidays, and cultural norms, ensuring that no team is disproportionately burdened or feels alienated due to their geographic location.

One of the key aspects of this principle is the recognition of the different rhythms and work cultures inherent in a global team. For instance, a team in India may start their day much earlier than their counterparts in the United States. Similarly, work-life balance expectations may vary significantly between teams in Europe and Asia. Respecting these differences and finding a middle ground where all team members can collaborate effectively is crucial for sustainable development.

To implement this principle, companies should consider flexible working arrangements that allow team members to work at times that suit them best, within the bounds of the project's requirements. This might involve staggered working hours, or setting core hours during which all team members are available for collaboration. Regular check-ins and open dialogue about workload and well-being can help in identifying and addressing any issues related to overwork or time zone challenges.

Another aspect is the adaptation of agile methodologies to fit a global context. This could involve adjusting sprint lengths, redefining the timing of stand-ups, or using asynchronous communication for updates and progress sharing. The goal is to ensure that agile practices, such as Scrum or Kanban, are applied in a way that respects the diverse working conditions of a global team.

Moreover, it's important to cultivate an inclusive work culture that values the contributions of all team members, regardless of their location. This includes providing equal opportunities for professional development, recognizing achievements, and ensuring that all voices are heard and valued during decision-making processes.

In summary, the updated principle emphasizes the need to adapt agile processes to the realities of a globally distributed team. By doing so, companies can maintain a sustainable pace of development that respects the diverse needs and work cultures of their global workforce, ultimately leading to more effective and harmonious team dynamics.

Pursue Technical Excellence with a Global Perspective

Original: "Continuous attention to technical excellence and good design enhances agility."

Updated: "Pursue technical excellence with a global perspective, leveraging diverse skills and insights."

The updated Agile principle, "Pursue technical excellence with a global perspective, leveraging diverse skills and insights," underlines the importance of embracing a wide-ranging approach to technical expertise in the context of software development outsourcing. This principle evolves from the original agile focus on technical excellence and good design by incorporating the diverse skills and perspectives that a global team can offer.

In the realm of outsourcing, technical excellence is not confined to just the mastery of programming languages or adherence to coding standards. It extends to understanding and integrating diverse methodologies, technologies, and perspectives from around the world. Each region or country brings its unique approach to problem-solving, innovation, and creativity in software development. By tapping into this rich tapestry of global talent, a company can significantly enhance the technical robustness and innovative capacity of its software products.

The principle emphasizes the need to actively seek and integrate these diverse skills and insights into the development process. It encourages the collaboration of experts from different geographical locations and cultural backgrounds, creating an environment where novel ideas and approaches are not only welcomed but actively sought out. This global perspective can lead to breakthroughs in design, functionality, and user experience, which might not be achievable with a more homogenous team.

Implementing this principle involves creating channels for knowledge exchange and collaboration among team members from different parts of the world. This could be through cross-regional workshops, joint problem-solving sessions, or shared online platforms where team members can contribute ideas, share best practices, and learn from each other's experiences. Regular knowledge-sharing sessions can be especially beneficial, allowing team members to stay abreast of the latest technological advancements and innovative practices in different regions.

Another key aspect is fostering a culture of continuous learning and improvement. Encouraging team members to pursue further training, certifications, and attend global conferences can help keep the team at the forefront of technological advancements. In addition, providing opportunities for team members to work on diverse projects across different regions can expose them to a variety of challenges and learning experiences, further enhancing their technical proficiency and adaptability.

The principle also entails respecting and valuing the diverse technical opinions and approaches within the team. This respect for diversity can lead to more creative solutions and a more robust design process, as different viewpoints and experiences are considered during the development phase.

In conclusion, by pursuing technical excellence with a global perspective and leveraging the diverse skills and insights of a multinational team, companies can significantly enhance the agility and innovation capacity of their software development processes. This approach not only improves the quality of the software produced but also contributes to a more inclusive, collaborative, and dynamic work environment.

Simplify Workflows Across Different Regions

Original: "Simplicity--the art of maximizing the amount of work not done--is essential."

Updated: "Simplify workflows and processes to enhance efficiency across different regions."

The revised Agile principle, "Simplify workflows and processes to enhance efficiency across different regions," takes on a deeper significance in the context of offshore outsourcing. It highlights the critical importance of streamlining infrastructure, processes, and communication channels to accommodate the complexities of working across diverse regions, countries, and languages. This principle is not just about reducing unnecessary work; it's about strategically designing systems and practices that can adapt to various global contexts without becoming overly complex or burdensome.

When applying this principle in practice, companies must consider the unique challenges of cross-regional collaboration. This involves ensuring that technological infrastructure is robust and accessible to all team members, regardless of their location. It means creating processes that are clear and straightforward, yet flexible enough to cater to the diverse working styles and cultural norms of a global team. Crucially, communication channels must be established that bridge language barriers and time zone differences, facilitating clear and continuous dialogue.

Simplifying in this context requires a thoughtful balance. It's about finding the most effective way to collaborate globally without imposing excessive administrative overhead or losing sight of the local nuances that can impact team dynamics and project outcomes. This approach not only makes working across borders more manageable but also ensures that the essence of Agile – speed, flexibility, and responsiveness – is preserved in a global setting.

Self-Organizing Teams with Cross-Cultural Dynamics

Original: "The best architectures, requirements, and designs emerge from self-organizing teams."

Updated: "Encourage self-organizing teams that respect and integrate cross-cultural dynamics."

The updated Agile principle, "Encourage self-organizing teams that respect and integrate cross-cultural dynamics," reflects a progressive approach to software development in the context of outsourcing. This principle underlines the importance of embracing the diverse cultural backgrounds and perspectives that team members from different geographical locations bring to the table. By mixing members from various regions, a richer, more nuanced understanding of the project and its potential impact across different cultures is fostered, ultimately leading to more robust and globally-relevant software solutions.

The process of integrating cross-cultural dynamics into a team isn't without its challenges, particularly in the initial stages where team members may need to navigate communication barriers and differing work styles. However, the long-term benefits of such diversity are invaluable, providing a well-rounded perspective that enhances creativity and problem-solving.

Furthermore, this principle emphasizes the need to move away from micromanagement, especially prevalent in outsourced team management due to trust issues. Instead, it advocates for empowering teams to self-organize and make decisions independently. This autonomy is crucial for fostering an environment where continuous improvement and innovation are not just encouraged but ingrained in the team's ethos.

In practice, this means providing teams with the necessary tools and support, and then trusting them to manage their workflows, make strategic decisions, and find solutions to challenges as they arise. Such an environment respects the unique contributions of each team member and leverages their collective expertise, regardless of their location. This shift from a control-centric to a trust-centric approach is pivotal in realizing the full potential of Agile in a global outsourcing context.

Empowering outsourced teams to autonomously select their colleagues, particularly for Junior and Mid-level positions, epitomizes the deep trust and mutual respect cultivated between the contracting firm and the outsourced team. This approach is underpinned by a shared understanding that the success of the project hinges not on individual prowess but on collective team performance. Therefore, it's in the team's best interest to choose members who align with the team's ethos and contribute to its overarching goals. This level of autonomy and responsibility, while requiring a foundational trust and established accountability, can significantly enhance team dynamics and project outcomes, fostering a more integrated and committed team environment.

Regular Reflection and Adjustment Across Time Zones

Original: "At regular intervals, the team reflects on how to become more effective, then tunes and adjusts its behavior accordingly."

Updated: "Teams, regardless of location, should regularly reflect and adapt, considering the dynamics of different time zones and cultures."

In the context of software development outsourcing, the updated Agile principle "Teams, regardless of location, should regularly reflect and adapt, considering the dynamics of different time zones and cultures," plays a crucial role. This principle emphasizes the importance of regular introspection and adjustment by teams, acknowledging the unique challenges posed by geographical and cultural differences.

The essence of this principle lies in promoting an environment where self-organizing teams, irrespective of their geographic location, are encouraged to engage in honest and open reflection. This process involves assessing their workflows, communication strategies, and project management techniques, with a focus on how these elements are influenced by varying time zones and cultural backgrounds. It's about understanding the nuances of working in a globally distributed team and using these insights to drive improvements in collaboration and efficiency.

Honest candor is vital in this context. It means creating a safe space where team members can freely express their thoughts, concerns, and suggestions without fear of reprisal or judgment. This open communication is key to identifying issues that might be unique to remote or culturally diverse teams, such as misunderstandings arising from language barriers or differing interpretations of work practices.

Additionally, this principle underscores the importance of organizing actionable plans for teams to hold themselves accountable. It's not just about identifying areas for improvement but also about setting clear, achievable goals and regularly reviewing progress towards these goals. This approach ensures that the reflections and discussions translate into tangible actions and measurable enhancements in team performance.

By fostering a culture of regular reflection and adaptation, taking into account the varied dynamics of a globally distributed team, organizations can ensure that their outsourced software development efforts are as effective and productive as possible. This continuous improvement cycle not only enhances the quality of the software developed but also contributes to a more harmonious and productive working relationship across borders.

Leveraging Diversity to Drive Product Innovation

Leveraging diversity in software development, especially in the context of outsourcing, is a powerful catalyst for driving product innovation. Diverse organizations, enriched by a variety of perspectives and experiences, have been consistently proven to be more innovative and better equipped to meet the multifaceted needs of their customers. While I don't have access to real-time data or specific statistics, numerous studies have highlighted the positive correlation between diversity and innovation.

When it comes to software development, diversity isn't just about having a mix of backgrounds in terms of ethnicity, gender, or age; it's also about embracing geographical, cultural, and experiential diversity. Outsourcing provides an unparalleled opportunity to tap into a global talent pool, bringing together individuals from different cities, countries, and continents, each with their own unique insights, problem-solving approaches, and creative ideas.

This amalgamation of varied perspectives is particularly potent in the tech industry, where innovation thrives on the exchange of ideas and the challenging of norms. Developers from different parts of the world not only speak different languages and consume different media, but they also interact with technology in distinct ways based on their local contexts and cultural influences. For instance, the way a software tool is used and perceived in one country might differ greatly from its use in another, leading to diverse user requirements and expectations.

By incorporating these wide-ranging perspectives into the development process, companies can create more nuanced, adaptable, and user-centric software products. For example, a team member in India might offer insights into how digital payments are evolving in the South Asian market, while a colleague in Brazil might have a deep understanding of social media trends in Latin America. Combining these insights with the technological expertise of developers from Silicon Valley or the startup mindset of a team in Eastern Europe can lead to breakthrough innovations that a homogenous team might never conceive.

Furthermore, the diversity in thought and background often leads to more creative problem-solving. Teams that are culturally diverse have been found to consider a wider range of solutions to a problem, as each member brings their unique set of experiences and knowledge to the table. This diversity of thought can be particularly beneficial in identifying and addressing unmet customer needs, leading to products that are not only innovative but also highly tailored to diverse user groups.

In summary, leveraging diversity in outsourced software development teams isn't just a good practice for fostering an inclusive work environment; it's a strategic imperative for companies seeking to stay competitive and innovative in the fast-paced tech industry. By embracing the rich tapestry of global perspectives, companies can drive product innovation, better meet the needs of a global customer base, and ultimately, achieve greater success in the market.

Leveraging Diversity to Drive Engineering Excellent

Leveraging diversity to drive engineering excellence is a crucial strategy in the realm of software development, particularly when teams are geographically dispersed. The essence of this approach lies in the recognition that diverse perspectives, stemming from differences in age, gender, cultural background, and geographical location, can significantly enhance problem-solving capabilities and innovative potential of engineering teams.

Consider the scenario of a 56-year-old male engineer from Birmingham, Alabama, and a 23-year-old female engineer from Manila, Philippines. Their distinct life experiences, cultural contexts, and educational backgrounds will inevitably shape their approach to problem-solving in unique ways. The senior engineer might bring decades of industry experience and a deep understanding of legacy systems, while the younger engineer could offer fresh insights into emerging technologies and contemporary user experiences. This diversity in perspective is not just advantageous; it's a powerful tool that can lead to more creative, robust, and effective engineering solutions.

When these diverse individuals are part of geographically dispersed engineering communities, the benefits are amplified. Each member brings not only their personal expertise but also the collective wisdom and strengths of their respective communities. For example, an engineer in Silicon Valley might be at the forefront of cutting-edge technology and startup culture, while an engineer in Bangalore, India, might have deep expertise in scalable software solutions and agile methodologies. By collaborating, these engineers pool their knowledge and resources, creating a synergy that transcends geographical boundaries.

This global network effect means that teams gain early exposure to global trends, diverse approaches to technology stacks, and varied design patterns and architectures. This exposure can be particularly advantageous when tackling complex, multifaceted problems. With a broader pool of ideas and experiences to draw from, teams are more likely to find innovative solutions that a more homogenous group might overlook.

However, to fully harness the potential of this diversity, open communication channels and a culture of honest and candid discussion are essential. Encouraging engineers to share their insights, challenge assumptions, and contribute their unique viewpoints is key to fostering an inclusive and dynamic team environment. This approach not only enhances problem-solving but also nurtures a culture of continuous learning and improvement.

In conclusion, leveraging diversity in engineering teams is not just about bringing together people from different backgrounds. It's about creating an environment where these differences are valued and harnessed to drive engineering excellence. By embracing a global perspective, encouraging open communication, and tapping into the collective wisdom of geographically dispersed communities, companies can build stronger, more innovative engineering teams capable of tackling the complex challenges of today's tech landscape.

Leveraging Time Zones to Drive Time to Market

In today's fast-paced market, leveraging time zones in software development can be a strategic asset for companies aiming to accelerate their time to market. This approach, often termed "Follow the Sun," exploits the natural progression of the day across different regions to maximize productivity and reduce development time for high-value customer features.

Imagine a scenario where a software development project is estimated to take 21 days for completion by a single team. Now, consider the same project being undertaken by three teams located in different time zones – say, the United States, Eastern Europe, and China. Each team works during their standard business hours, passing off their work to the next team as their day ends and another begins. This relay can potentially reduce the completion time to just 7-9 days, depending on the efficiency of integration and handover processes.

The underlying principle of this approach is simple yet powerful: as one team winds down for the day, another team, in a different time zone, picks up where they left off. This continuous cycle of development ensures that the project is progressing around the clock, significantly reducing the overall development time. This method doesn't just expedite delivery; it also taps into the peak productive hours of each team, ensuring quality output.

However, the successful implementation of the "Follow the Sun" model hinges on several factors. Effective communication and meticulous planning are paramount to ensure seamless handovers between teams. This involves clear documentation, regular updates, and synchronization meetings to align on progress and expectations. Technology plays a crucial role here, with tools for collaboration, version control, and real-time communication being integral to the process.

The competitive advantage of this model is substantial. In a market where speed and agility are crucial, being able to innovate and iterate up to three times faster than competitors can significantly impact a company's market position. This speed allows for quicker response to customer feedback, faster delivery of new features, and the ability to pivot rapidly in response to market changes.

In the later sections of this book, we will delve deeper into the "Follow the Sun" methodology, discussing frameworks and best practices for its effective implementation. This will include strategies for overcoming common challenges such as cultural differences, communication barriers, and maintaining consistent quality standards across globally distributed teams. By mastering this approach, companies can turn the challenge of time zone differences into a strategic advantage, driving faster time to market and staying ahead in the competitive landscape of software development.

The Agile Outsourcing Baby Steps (CRAFTS)

As we delve deeper into the intricacies of outsourcing and the fundamental principles of agile methodologies tailored for this context, we arrive at a crucial juncture: the practical implementation of Agile Outsourcing. Transitioning from in-house software development to a model that harnesses the continuous, around-the-clock productivity offered by global outsourcing requires a structured approach. This is where the CRAFTS method comes into play. CRAFTS provides a comprehensive blueprint for navigating the shift from traditional in-house development to an effective Agile Outsourcing model.

It's important to note that the application of the CRAFTS method is a post-selection strategy. In other words, this framework is most effective once you have identified and engaged with your outsourcing partners – a topic we will explore in greater detail in a later section of this book. The essence of CRAFTS is to ensure a seamless integration of outsourced teams into your existing workflows and to leverage their capabilities in harmony with your agile practices.

By adhering to the CRAFTS method, organizations can effectively bridge the gap between the potential of outsourcing and the agile ethos, achieving a synthesis that brings out the best in both worlds. It's a journey that demands careful planning, clear communication, and a deep understanding of both agile principles and the dynamics of outsourcing. This method is not just about offloading work; it's about creating a synergistic relationship between in-house and outsourced teams, fostering an environment where continuous innovation, efficiency, and quality are at the forefront.

The CRAFTS Method

Code delivery capability

Responsive Agile culture.

Adopt Agile processes.

Fully integrated Team Ownership.

Tireless Continuous Improvement.

Synchronized work

C - Code Delivery Capability

The cornerstone of effective outsourcing in software development is the inherent ability to deliver software independently. This means having a robust understanding and practical experience in the complete lifecycle of software development - from requirement gathering and coding to deployment, monitoring, and customer support. It's crucial that before venturing into outsourcing, organizations must be adept in these competencies internally to set the stage for successful collaboration with outsourced teams.

R - Responsive Agile Culture

Agile is not just a methodology; it's a culture that needs to permeate an organization. Establishing a responsive Agile culture involves embracing a philosophy of achieving significant goals in small, manageable increments. It's about fostering an environment that values continuous improvement and innovation, encouraging teams to adapt swiftly to changing requirements and market conditions. This cultural shift is vital for aligning outsourced teams with the company's agile practices and overall business strategy.

A - Adopt Agile Processes

Implementing Agile processes is key to harmonizing workflows between onshore and outsourced teams. This involves establishing a predictable and yet flexible software development process that enables continuous or bi-weekly delivery of code to production. A well-defined workflow for managing bugs, support, and feedback, coupled with open communication channels, ensures that outsourced teams are fully integrated into the development lifecycle, enhancing efficiency and product quality.

F - Fully Integrated Team Ownership

Taking ownership of the teams you hire, whether in-house or outsourced, is fundamental. This element advocates for treating all engineers equally, irrespective of their employment status or location. Fully integrated team ownership means breaking down barriers between 'us' and 'them,' fostering a unified team ethos. It involves getting to know your outsourced team members, including them in product planning, giving them access to customers and key metrics, and allowing them to share both the successes and challenges.

T - Tireless Continuous Improvement

The journey towards outsourcing excellence is continuous. This step emphasizes the importance of constantly refining and enhancing both processes and products. It involves a proactive stance towards improving methodologies, technologies, and practices, ensuring that the outsourced strategy remains aligned with the evolving business goals and market demands.

S - Synchronized Work

Once the fundamentals are firmly established, organizations can advance to a 'Follow the Sun' model. This approach leverages global time differences to enable 24-hour development cycles. By breaking down large projects into smaller units and employing standardized processes, automated testing, and CI/CD, organizations can synchronize work across global teams. This method maximizes productivity and accelerates project timelines, turning the geographical spread of teams into a strategic advantage.

In summary, "CRAFTS" is a strategic framework designed to guide organizations through the complexities of outsourcing in software development. It encompasses the essential principles and practices needed to build, manage, and evolve successful outsourced engagements. By adhering to the "CRAFTS" model, organizations can navigate the challenges of outsourcing with skill and precision, transforming global team dynamics into a cohesive, efficient, and innovative force driving software excellence.

C - Code Delivery Capability

In this initial section, we're going to have a candid discussion about the fundamental aspect of software development: Code Delivery Capability. This is an introspective moment for you, regardless of the size of your development team—whether it's a compact group of five, a robust hundred, or an expansive thousand engineers. The questions we need to address here are straightforward yet profound:

1. Are you consistently and regularly shipping your product?
2. Are you building a product that truly aligns with your customers' needs and market demands?
3. Are you able to maintain high standards of quality in your software?

These questions are not just rhetorical checkpoints; they are the pillars upon which successful software development stands. The ability to deliver code effectively is what separates thriving projects from those that languish in perceptual development. If your team is struggling with these aspects, it's a crucial time to reassess your approach. We will delve into the essential skill sets needed to enhance your code delivery capability. If you find that these challenges are persistent and hampering your progress, you might need to reconsider your strategy. It could be more beneficial to opt for project-based outsourcing to a specialized vendor, rather than sticking with staff augmentation. This decision could be the turning point in how you approach the development and delivery of your software.

Collect & Manage the Requirements of your Software

In the realm of software development, the ability to effectively collect and manage requirements is paramount. This process is not just about gathering information; it's about ensuring that these requirements genuinely reflect the expectations and needs of your customers. Let's break down what this involves:

Firstly, there's the collection of requirements directly from customers. This step is crucial as it sets the stage for everything that follows. It's not just about what customers say they want; it's about understanding their underlying needs and how your software can meet them.

Once these requirements are gathered, the next step is ensuring they align with what customers actually expect. This involves a delicate balance of technical feasibility, business strategy, and user experience. It's about finding the sweet spot where customer expectations, business goals, and technological capabilities intersect.

Prioritization of these requirements is another critical aspect. With numerous requests and limited resources, focusing on high-priority tasks ensures that the most impactful features are developed first. This process requires a deep understanding of both the market demands and the strategic direction of the product.

The ability to estimate the cost of software is a critical skill to ensure the company's money is being well spent. It does not make good financial sense to write software that costs 10 or 20 times the cost of expected revenue when the company will never recoup this investment. There must be the ability to calculate, and track, ROI, even down to the feature level.

Breaking down large requests into manageable chunks is another skill that cannot be overstated. Large, complex requirements can be overwhelming and unmanageable. Decomposing these into smaller, more manageable tasks not only makes the development process smoother but also allows for more flexibility and adaptability in the development cycle.

Translating customer requirements into formats that are consumable for development teams, such as user stories, is a key skill. This translation ensures that the development team clearly understands what needs to be built and the context behind it. User stories act as a bridge between the non-technical language of the customer and the technical language of the developers.

Tracking larger projects is also essential. It's not enough to break down and start working on tasks; you need to have a clear overview of the project's progress. This involves monitoring development stages, managing timelines, and ensuring that every piece aligns with the larger goal.

Lastly, projecting the completion of larger projects is a crucial capability. Stakeholders, be it internal or external, often require estimates on when a project or a major feature will be completed. This requires not only a deep understanding of the project scope but also the ability to accurately estimate timelines considering various factors like team capacity, technical challenges, and external dependencies.

Mastering these aspects of requirement collection and management is fundamental in ensuring that your software development is not just efficient, but also effectively aligned with your customers' needs and your business objectives.

Build Your Software

When it comes to software development, especially in an outsourced environment, the translation of requirements into functional, maintainable, and high-quality software is a critical process. Let's delve into what this encompasses:

First and foremost, the development team must possess a deep understanding of the requirements. This comprehension goes beyond the superficial acceptance of a task; it involves grasping the underlying business logic and the intended outcomes. The team should be able to connect the dots between what is asked for and why it's needed, which is pivotal for successful implementation.

Alignment between what is built by the development team and what is expected by product management is crucial. This requires ongoing communication and checks to ensure that the development is on track with the product vision. Discrepancies here can lead to costly reworks and delays.

The ability to write working code is fundamental. However, it's not just about creating code that functions; it's about crafting code that is robust, efficient, and aligns with the project's objectives. The team should strive to produce code that does what it's supposed to do without unforeseen issues or bugs.

Writing maintainable code is a fundamental aspect of sustainable software development. The goal is to create software that not only fulfills current requirements but is also agile enough to accommodate future changes and enhancements. This necessitates a focus on clean, modular, and scalable coding practices. Such code is characterized by its clarity, logical structure, and the use of well-defined modules that can be updated or replaced independently without affecting the overall system. It's about anticipating the need for change and preparing the codebase in a way that simplifies these future modifications. Employing these practices ensures that the software remains robust, versatile, and responsive to evolving business needs or technological advancements. By prioritizing maintainability, developers create a foundation that supports continuous improvement and adaptation, key attributes in a dynamic technological landscape.

The clarity of code is another key aspect. Developers should write code that is understandable, not just to themselves but to anyone else who might work on it in the future. This involves clear structuring, logical flow, and adherence to standard coding practices.

Documenting architecture and major technical decisions is crucial in software development, particularly when it involves scalability. Such documentation serves as a vital roadmap for both current and future development teams, offering comprehensive insights into the architectural framework and the reasoning behind significant technical choices. It elucidates the structural design, illustrates how various components of the system interact, and explains why specific technologies or approaches were selected. This information is invaluable in guiding ongoing development and facilitating future modifications or enhancements. It ensures that the team's collective knowledge and strategic thinking are preserved, enabling subsequent developers to understand the context of the existing architecture. This understanding is essential for maintaining the integrity and efficacy of the system as it evolves, ensuring that scalability and other key considerations remain central to the development process.

Effective management of source control is a fundamental aspect of modern software development, crucial for maintaining the integrity and evolution of codebases over time. A proficient software development team must possess the capability to expertly navigate source control systems. This involves organizing code in a structured and accessible manner, ensuring that changes made by different team members are seamlessly integrated without conflict. It also includes maintaining a clear history of code changes, which is invaluable for tracking progress, understanding past decisions, and troubleshooting issues. Good source control management fosters collaborative development, allowing multiple developers to work concurrently on different aspects of a project while minimizing the risk of overlapping work or version conflicts. It's not just about storing code; it's about managing the development process in a way that enhances efficiency, reduces errors, and maintains a high standard of code quality. In essence, adept source control management is the backbone of a cohesive and productive software development team, ensuring smooth progression from concept to deployment.

Writing well-written and readable code is a vital skill in software development, crucial for maintaining high standards of code quality. It entails adhering to established coding conventions, which are essentially agreed-upon guidelines within a development team or the wider developer community. These conventions might include specific practices regarding naming conventions, indentation, commenting, and structuring of code. The logical organization of code is also paramount. It ensures that the codebase is intuitive and easy to navigate, making it easier for other developers, including future team members, to understand and build upon the existing work. Simplicity is another key aspect; it involves writing code that is straightforward and avoids unnecessary complexity, making it more accessible and reducing the likelihood of errors. Well-written and readable code not only facilitates smoother collaboration and maintenance but also accelerates the process of debugging and enhances the overall scalability of the software. In summary, the art of crafting well-written and readable code is about creating a clear, consistent, and maintainable codebase that stands the test of time and teamwork.

Well-commented code plays a critical role, especially in environments where collaboration and outsourcing are prevalent. Effective comments in the code serve as a roadmap, offering vital context and explanations. They elucidate the purpose behind specific segments of code, making the intentions of the developer clear. This is particularly important when dealing with complex logic or intricate algorithms, where the reasoning behind certain decisions might not be immediately apparent. Comments should be concise yet informative, guiding any team member, regardless of their familiarity with the code, to a deeper understanding of its functionality. This practice transforms the codebase into a more accessible, user-friendly resource, ensuring that everyone, from in-house developers to outsourced teams, can work efficiently and cohesively. Well-commented code not only eases maintenance and future modifications but also fosters a more inclusive and collaborative development environment.

Adherence to security expectations in coding is an essential, non-negotiable aspect of software development. It is imperative for the team to possess a robust understanding of and commitment to implementing security best practices. This involves more than just a superficial application of security measures; it requires a deep understanding of the potential vulnerabilities and threats specific to the technology stack being used. The team must be proficient in identifying and mitigating risks, ensuring that the code they write is not just functional but also secure from potential breaches. This skill set is crucial in today's digital landscape, where security threats are increasingly sophisticated and pervasive. By embedding security considerations into the coding process, the team can safeguard the software against vulnerabilities, ensuring the integrity and reliability of the product they are developing. This approach is fundamental in building and maintaining trust with users and stakeholders, as it demonstrates a commitment to protecting their data and privacy.

The team should also have the ability to write code that is maintainable and expandable by more than one person. This collaborative approach ensures that the codebase doesn't become too reliant on a single developer and can be efficiently worked on by any qualified team member.

The ability to write usable software is a critical aspect of software development, central to the success and adoption of any application. Usability encompasses designing software with an intuitive and user-friendly interface, ensuring that end-users can effortlessly navigate and utilize its features. The core of usability lies in understanding the users' needs and perspectives, translating them into a design that feels natural and straightforward. Even the most technically robust software can fail to meet its objectives if users struggle to understand or operate it. Therefore, the development process must prioritize user experience (UX) at every stage, from the initial design to the final product. This involves iterative testing, user feedback, and a keen focus on the simplicity and clarity of the user interface. A software that aligns well with user expectations and behaviors not only enhances user satisfaction but also encourages wider adoption and more effective utilization, ultimately determining the software's overall success.

Finally, staying within cost estimations is a critical part of software development. The team should be skilled at managing resources, time, and effort to ensure that the project doesn't exceed its budget. This requires a keen understanding of cost factors and efficient project management practices.

In summary, the ability to translate requirements into working software encompasses a range of skills and practices. It's about understanding, clarity, maintainability, security, and efficiency, all while keeping an eye on the cost and overall project goals.

Test Your Software

Incorporating quality into software products is a multifaceted process that requires a comprehensive approach to testing and validation. Let's explore the essential elements that software development teams must consider to ensure they are building quality into their products:

Firstly, it is imperative to write code that is fully tested against the requirements. This means every piece of code should be verified to meet the specified criteria and functionality. Testing against requirements ensures that the final product aligns with the client's expectations and the project's goals.

Automated unit testing is a crucial aspect of quality assurance. It involves testing individual units or components of the software to ensure they function correctly in isolation. Unit tests are typically written and maintained by the developers themselves and are run frequently to catch issues early in the development cycle.

In addition to unit testing, automated integration testing is vital. This testing phase focuses on the interactions between different modules or services in the application. It helps identify any integration issues that might occur when individual units are combined.

End-to-end automated testing is another key component. This type of testing simulates real user scenarios to ensure that the entire application, from start to finish, functions as expected. It covers the application's overall workflow and is essential for verifying the user experience.

Performance testing is critical for assessing the software's efficiency and responsiveness. It involves testing the application under various loads to ensure it performs optimally and can handle the expected user traffic without significant slowdowns or crashes.

Security review and testing are non-negotiable in today's digital landscape. This involves scrutinizing the code for vulnerabilities and potential security threats. It's crucial to conduct thorough security assessments and penetration testing to safeguard the application against potential attacks and breaches.

There must be processes in place to correct or deprioritize bugs found within the quality process. It must not be acceptable to throw bugs over the fence or deploy code with known quality issues that have not been fixed or negotiated with the product manager.

Finally, ensuring that new code does not break other features within the application is essential for maintaining a stable and reliable software product. This requires rigorous regression testing to check that new changes or additions do not adversely affect existing functionalities.

In summary, building quality into software products demands a comprehensive testing strategy that includes unit, integration, end-to-end, performance, and security testing. This approach ensures that the software is robust, secure, performs well under varying conditions, and provides a seamless user experience without compromising existing functionalities.

Deploy Your Software

Deploying code to production is a critical capability for any software development team, encapsulating several crucial skills and procedures to ensure that updates are delivered smoothly, effectively, and without disruption to the end-users. This process is not just about pushing new code; it involves a comprehensive approach to managing various aspects of the deployment process. Here's an elaboration on the necessary abilities:

The team must be proficient in packaging and deploying code to the production environment. This involves understanding how to compile code, manage dependencies, and handle versioning to ensure that the deployed code is stable and reliable.

In addition to code, the team needs to effectively manage database changes. This includes the ability to create scripts for database migrations and update the database schema without losing data or causing downtime.

For applications that rely heavily on data, the team must also have the capability to manage and deploy data changes. This involves ensuring data integrity and consistency across different versions and environments.

Content management is another crucial aspect, especially for content-driven applications. The team should be able to update and deploy new content efficiently, ensuring that it aligns with the application's functionality and user expectations.

Configuring various environments is a foundational skill. Teams must set up and manage development, staging, and production environments, ensuring each environment is correctly configured and mimics real-world conditions as closely as possible.

Before deploying to production, the ability to deploy to lower environments, such as development and staging, is vital. This allows the team to test the deployment process, identify potential issues, and ensure that the application behaves as expected in a controlled setting.

Deployment isn't without risks, and the ability to roll back deployments is essential. The team should have strategies and tools in place to quickly revert changes in the event of a deployment causing issues in the production environment.

Finally, monitoring and verifying deployments are critical. The team should be able to track the deployment process, quickly identify and resolve any issues that arise, and confirm that the deployment has been successful and that the application is performing optimally in the production environment.

Each of these abilities is crucial in ensuring that software updates are delivered efficiently, securely, and with minimal disruption, thus contributing to a robust and reliable software development lifecycle.

Operate Your Software

Operating software in production, particularly for SaaS or mobile applications, encompasses a range of critical competencies that ensure the application's effectiveness and reliability.

The capability to serve the application to its intended audiences is fundamental. This involves ensuring that the application is accessible to its users, regardless of their location or device, and that it meets their specific needs and expectations. This requires a deep understanding of the audience's characteristics and preferences, as well as the technical ability to optimize the application for various platforms and user conditions.

Equally important is the ability to serve the application in a performant manner. Performance is key to user satisfaction and engagement. This entails optimizing load times, ensuring efficient data handling, and providing a seamless and responsive user experience. Teams need to balance the technical demands of the application with the hardware and network capabilities of their target audience.

Monitoring production for quality issues is vital to maintain the application's health and user satisfaction. This involves setting up effective systems to continuously track the application's performance, identify bugs or glitches, and implement timely fixes. Effective quality monitoring helps in pre-empting user complaints and ensures that the application remains reliable and trustworthy.

Security monitoring in production is non-negotiable. With increasing cyber threats, it is crucial to have robust systems in place to detect and mitigate potential security breaches. This requires ongoing vigilance and the use of advanced security tools and practices to protect user data and maintain trust.

Logging user activities serves multiple purposes. For support, it helps in troubleshooting and resolving user issues effectively. It provides a historical record of user interactions with the application, which is invaluable in diagnosing and fixing problems. For product management, these logs offer insights into user behavior, preferences, and pain points, informing future product development and enhancements.

Disaster recovery capabilities are a must. This means having strategies and tools in place to quickly recover from catastrophic events, whether they are system failures, data breaches, or natural disasters. Effective disaster recovery plans minimize downtime and data loss, ensuring business continuity and safeguarding user trust.

The ability to scale the application in response to varying user demand is crucial for maintaining performance levels. This requires a flexible architecture and infrastructure that can adapt to changes in load, ensuring that the application remains stable and responsive even under heavy use.

Finally, the ability to report and manage costs related to hosting the software is a key operational skill. This involves optimizing resource utilization and costs, ensuring that the hosting infrastructure is both efficient and cost-effective, without compromising on the quality and reliability of the service provided.

Together, these skills ensure that the application is not only functionally effective but also reliable, secure, and cost-efficient, providing a positive and consistent experience for its users.

Support Your Software

Supporting software in production is a multi-faceted task, demanding a range of skills to ensure efficient and effective customer service.

The first crucial ability is for customers to reach support staff easily. This involves establishing clear and accessible communication channels, such as email, phone, chat, or a ticketing system. The goal is to make it straightforward for customers to report issues or seek help, thus enhancing their experience and satisfaction with the product.

Next, it's essential for support staff to have access to the customer data necessary to assist them effectively. This requires a system that safely and efficiently provides relevant user data, such as user settings, transaction history, or error logs. Access to this data enables support staff to understand the issue fully and provide informed and accurate assistance.

The ability of support staff to resolve customer issues is paramount. This involves not only technical knowledge and problem-solving skills but also an understanding of the product's nuances and user needs. Staff should be trained and equipped to handle a wide range of queries and problems, ensuring quick and satisfactory resolutions for the customers.

Keeping support staff informed about the product and new features as they're released is equally important. Continuous training and updates ensure that the team is knowledgeable about the latest developments and functionalities, enabling them to provide accurate and relevant information to users.

The ability to escalate issues to more technical resources is a key aspect of effective support. Some customer issues may require deeper technical investigation or intervention. The support team should have clear escalation protocols and access to technical experts when needed, ensuring that complex issues are handled efficiently and expertly.

Being able to submit bugs, track them, and report back to customers when they are resolved, is a critical function of a support team. This involves not just logging issues but also monitoring their progress through the development cycle and keeping the customer informed. This transparency and communication build trust and confidence in the product and the company.

Lastly, the support team's ability to provide feedback and ideas on the product that can be used to fix and enhance the product by the product and development teams is invaluable. This frontline feedback is a goldmine of insights into user experiences and potential improvements. Encouraging and structuring this feedback loop can lead to significant enhancements in the product, ultimately benefiting both the users and the company.

Document Your Software

The necessity of comprehensive documentation in software development cannot be overstated, particularly in the context of outsourced teams. Effective documentation serves as a bridge between the software and its users, be they customers, support staff, or other developers. A key aspect of this is the simultaneous release of software and its accompanying documentation. This ensures that as soon as a product is available, users have access to necessary guides and support materials, enhancing their ability to utilize the software effectively.

Aligning the methodologies of the documentation team with those of the development teams is vital, particularly in agile environments. This alignment ensures that documentation evolves in tandem with the software, maintaining accuracy and relevance. Agile methodologies in documentation can facilitate quicker updates and more responsive changes, reflecting the dynamic nature of software development.

Moreover, the role of documentation in reducing the time to value for customers is significant. Well-crafted documentation can expedite the process of users understanding and deriving value from the software, enabling a holistic and accurate application of the solution. This aspect is particularly crucial in outsourced development, where direct communication between developers and end-users may be limited.

Lastly, compliance and regulatory mandates often require specific technical documentation to accompany software products. The ability to integrate these requirements seamlessly into the documentation process is essential. This not only ensures legal compliance but also adds a layer of trust and credibility to the software, particularly in industries with stringent regulatory standards. By mastering these aspects of software documentation, companies can ensure that their outsourced software development efforts are as effective and efficient as possible.

Train Users on Your Software

The skills involved in effectively training users on software is a crucial component of successful software deployment, particularly in the context of outsourced development where direct interaction with the development team may be limited. The training approach needs to be as diverse and adaptable as the users themselves, encompassing various methods to cater to different learning styles and requirements.

In-app guided tours represent an interactive and user-friendly approach to training, offering real-time guidance as users navigate the software. This method is particularly effective for new users or for introducing new features, as it provides immediate context and practical application.

Conferences and workshops, whether virtual or onsite, offer a more in-depth and comprehensive training experience. These sessions can be tailored to cover specific aspects of the software in detail and often provide an opportunity for direct interaction and feedback, which is invaluable for both users and developers.

Classes, another vital training tool, can be offered in various formats – from webinars to classroom settings. These can be designed to cater to different user groups, from beginners to advanced users, ensuring that each user can find the level of instruction they need. The flexibility to offer these classes virtually or onsite broadens their accessibility.

The business model around training can vary – it can be included as part of the software package, or offered as a separate, paid service. The choice largely depends on the software's complexity, the user's familiarity with similar products, and the company's business strategy.

Customized training solutions can also be offered, particularly for clients with unique requirements or for software that is highly specialized. This bespoke training ensures that the specific needs of each client are met, ensuring they get the most value from the software.

Ultimately, the goal of any training initiative is to empower users to fully understand and effectively utilize the software, maximizing the value they derive from it. Effective training not only enhances user satisfaction and proficiency but also reduces the burden on support teams and improves overall product adoption. For companies employing outsourced development teams, investing in a robust and varied training program is essential to ensure their end-users can fully leverage the software's capabilities.

Secure Your Software

The importance of building secure software in the modern SaaS or mobile application landscape cannot be overstated. As more businesses and consumers depend on these platforms for critical operations and personal transactions, ensuring their security is paramount. To effectively write secure software, there are six key areas that development teams need to focus on:

APIs are the linchpins in the architecture of SaaS applications, facilitating communication between various software components. Ensuring robust API security is crucial. This involves implementing measures to verify that only authorized entities and applications have access to your data, thus preventing unauthorized data exposure. Techniques like API gateways, token-based authentication, and rigorous access control mechanisms are essential to fortify API security.

Cybersecurity plays a critical role in the realm of identity and access management (IAM), particularly in the context of Software as a Service (SaaS) and mobile application development. IAM encompasses the processes and technologies used to control and manage user access to digital resources. In today's digital landscape, where data breaches and unauthorized access are prevalent threats, robust IAM solutions are imperative. For SaaS providers and mobile app developers, ensuring the security and privacy of user data is paramount. Effective IAM not only safeguards sensitive information but also enhances the user experience by enabling seamless yet secure access. By implementing strong authentication methods, role-based access control, and continuous monitoring, organizations can protect their applications and user identities, instilling trust and confidence among their user base while mitigating the risks associated with unauthorized access and data breaches. As the digital ecosystem continues to evolve, the importance of IAM in SaaS and mobile application development cannot be overstated, as it forms the foundation for secure, reliable, and user-friendly experiences.

In SaaS and mobile applications, data encryption is a fundamental security measure. Encrypting data converts it into a format that is unreadable without the corresponding decryption key. This practice is particularly critical for data in transit, as it traverses through various networks to reach the end user. By encrypting data, you ensure that even if it's intercepted or compromised, it remains indecipherable and secure from unauthorized access.

The management of data access is a vital element of software security.

Establishing comprehensive data access policies helps in governing who can access specific data and the extent of their interaction with it. These policies should clearly define user roles, set permissions, and outline robust authentication procedures. Regular reviews and updates to these policies are necessary to adapt to evolving business requirements and emerging security threats.

While we will go into this pillar in more detail in the next section, adherence to compliance standards is a critical aspect of SaaS security. Using compliance management tools, organizations can ensure their SaaS applications conform to various regulatory requirements. These tools facilitate essential functions like maintaining audit trails, enabling real-time monitoring, and generating automated compliance reports. This not only aids in simplifying the compliance process but also significantly reduces the risks of non-compliance penalties.

A comprehensive approach to disaster recovery and business continuity is integral to the resilience of SaaS platforms. Developing a disaster recovery plan involves identifying critical software components, setting recovery objectives, and establishing clear roles and responsibilities for recovery efforts. In parallel, a business continuity plan should focus on maintaining or swiftly resuming business-critical functions in the event of a disruption. This includes strategies for crisis communication, effective business process management, and workforce deployment during and after a disaster.

By addressing these six pillars, software development teams can ensure that their SaaS or mobile applications are not only functional and user-friendly but also secure and resilient against various cyber threats and operational disruptions. This holistic approach to security is indispensable in building trust with users and maintaining the integrity of digital platforms in an increasingly interconnected world.

Make Your Software Compliant

In today's technology-driven business environment, compliance with various regulatory frameworks and industry standards is not just a necessity but a significant aspect of establishing trust and ensuring security. Organizations, especially those engaging in outsourced software development, need to equip themselves with the right skill sets to effectively navigate and fulfill compliance requirements. This involves multiple stages, each demanding meticulous attention and expertise.

Defining the necessary controls within an organization is the foundational step. This requires a deep understanding of the relevant compliance frameworks, be it SOC 2 Type 2, HIPAA, FedRAMP, GDPR, or any other. Identifying and establishing these controls involves analyzing the specific needs and risks of the organization, and then tailoring controls that address these risks while adhering to the compliance requirements.

Once the controls are defined, the next crucial step is implementing them within the organization. This process involves not only the technical integration of these controls into the software and infrastructure but also ensuring that the organizational policies and procedures are aligned with these controls. Effective implementation requires a collaborative effort across various departments, including IT, legal, and compliance teams.

Testing these controls internally is an ongoing process and an integral part of compliance management. Regular internal audits and assessments ensure that the controls are functioning as intended and provide an opportunity to identify and rectify any gaps or weaknesses.

Having these controls audited by an external party is a critical step to validate compliance. This involves presenting the organizational controls and processes to an independent auditor who assesses their adequacy and effectiveness against the standards of the compliance framework.

Passing an audit is a significant milestone that demonstrates the organization's commitment to compliance and security. It requires thorough preparation, extensive documentation, and often, remediation efforts based on initial audit findings.

For organizations that are more advanced in their compliance journey, there's an opportunity to leverage technology for continuous compliance monitoring. Automated collection and testing of evidence can streamline the audit process and provide real-time insights into the compliance posture, significantly reducing the effort and time required for periodic audits.

Compliance, particularly in software development, spans various aspects including the software itself, the underlying infrastructure, organizational policies, and the people involved in the development and maintenance of the software. Consulting with a compliance advisor is advisable to ensure that your organization's compliance strategy is comprehensive and tailored to its specific needs and risks.

As software development increasingly involves global teams and outsourced partnerships, the ability to manage compliance effectively across different jurisdictions and regulatory environments becomes crucial. This not only helps in mitigating risks but also in building trust with clients and stakeholders, a key advantage in today's competitive marketplace.

Communicate Changes to Your Software

In the realm of software development, particularly when outsourcing is involved, effective communication skills are not just beneficial – it's essential. Effective communication encompasses a range of practices and competencies that ensure all necessary stakeholders, both internal and external, are kept in the loop, engaged, and aligned with the project's progress and objectives.

First and foremost, it's about maintaining regular and timely communication. This means not only updating stakeholders on the progress and milestones achieved but also proactively addressing potential issues or changes. Timely communication helps in managing expectations and ensures that everyone is on the same page, reducing the risks of misunderstandings or misalignments.

Furthermore, communication in software development extends beyond the immediate development team. It involves coordination with various other departments that play a role in the product's lifecycle. For example, aligning with the marketing team ensures that the product's features are accurately promoted. Collaborating with sales teams helps in understanding customer needs and feedback, which can be vital for product improvement. Finance and legal departments are crucial for budgeting, compliance, and addressing any contractual aspects of the project. Similarly, customer success teams can provide invaluable insights into user experiences and areas for enhancement.

Each of these departments has its own language and priorities, and effective communication involves translating technical aspects into a format that is understandable and relevant to them. It's about creating a dialogue that enables these departments to contribute to and benefit from the development process, enhancing the product's overall value and market fit.

In summary, the skillset around communication in outsourced software development involves more than just regular updates. It's about fostering a culture of open dialogue, understanding the needs and languages of different stakeholders, and ensuring that all departments involved in the product management process are actively engaged and contributing. This holistic approach to communication is critical in realizing the full potential of the software development process and delivering a product that meets and exceeds stakeholder expectations.

Track Your Software

In the dynamic landscape of software development, particularly for SaaS or mobile applications, the ability to track and analyze various metrics is crucial. This skillset extends beyond technical proficiency, encompassing financial, project management, and marketing aspects, which are vital for understanding the performance and impact of the software.

Firstly, financial metrics play a significant role in assessing the health and success of software, especially in a SaaS model. Key financial metrics include Customer Churn, which indicates the rate at which customers stop using the software, and Annual Recurring Revenue (ARR), a measure of the predictable and recurring revenue components. Revenue Churn, which tracks lost revenue from existing customers, alongside Customer Lifetime Value (CLV) and Customer Acquisition Cost (CAC), are essential for evaluating the long-term financial viability and customer retention strategies. The Months to Recover CAC and the CAC:LTV Ratio provide insights into the cost-effectiveness of customer acquisition and the return on investment.

In terms of agile project management, the ability to track specific metrics allows teams to assess their efficiency and adaptability. This includes monitoring sprint velocity, release frequency, and the backlog burn-down rate. These metrics provide a clear picture of the team's productivity and the progress made towards achieving project goals.

Furthermore, integrating software metrics with marketing metrics is vital in today's interconnected business environment. Metrics such as Qualified Marketing Traffic, Leads by Lifecycle Stage, and the Lead-to-Customer Rate offer valuable insights into how effectively the software attracts and converts potential customers. Additionally, the Customer Engagement Score and Customer Health Score are crucial for understanding user engagement and satisfaction, which can inform both product development and marketing strategies.

In summary, mastering the ability to track and interpret these diverse metrics is essential for any software development team, especially in an agile and customer-centric business model like SaaS. These metrics provide a comprehensive view of the software's performance, financial health, project management efficiency, and market impact, enabling informed decision-making and strategic planning. By leveraging these metrics effectively, teams can optimize their processes, enhance customer satisfaction, and ultimately drive the success of their software products.

Creating Software Summary

In the "Code Delivery Capability" section, we delve into the foundational competencies that a company must possess to effectively leverage outsourced software development resources. The journey begins with the ability to collect and manage requirements, ensuring that what is built aligns perfectly with customer expectations and is prioritized for maximum business impact.

Building upon this, a company must have the expertise to transform these requirements into robust, maintainable, and secure software. This includes a rigorous testing regime that not only validates functionality against requirements but also ensures performance, security, and compliance with regulatory standards.

Deploying the software is the next critical step, where the ability to package, configure, and release the application across various environments is tested. This step also includes the ability to monitor deployments and, if necessary, roll them back efficiently.

Operating the software in a live production environment demands a set of skills to ensure that the application is performant, scalable, and resilient against disasters, all while keeping a vigilant eye on security and quality metrics.

Supporting the software post-deployment is about ensuring that user issues are promptly and effectively resolved, with support staff having deep product knowledge and the ability to provide feedback to further refine the product.

Documentation and training users on the software go hand in hand to ensure that the software's value is fully realized by the end-users. Clear and comprehensive documentation supports this by providing guidance on the use and maintenance of the software.

Finally, a company's ability to track various metrics related to the software's financial performance, project management effectiveness, and market impact is essential for continuous improvement and alignment with business goals.

Once a company masters these capabilities, it can confidently harness the power of outsourced resources, knowing that it has the necessary infrastructure and processes to ensure the delivery of high-quality software products.

When a company finds itself not mature enough in any of the critical areas necessary for successful software delivery, the path forward requires a strategic, inward focus. The company must prioritize internal development of these core capabilities before considering an expansion into outsourcing. This could mean investing time and resources to cultivate these skills within the existing workforce or perhaps slowing down the pace to ensure that the foundational practices are solid and repeatable.

In some cases, bringing in seasoned management with a track record of delivering software at the desired level of maturity can catalyze the necessary changes. These leaders can implement best practices, mentor existing teams, and instill a culture of excellence and continuous improvement.

Alternatively, if immediate progress is necessary and internal development isn't feasible, a company may opt to partner with an outsourced vendor that not only provides development services but also excels in the areas where the company lacks maturity. The right vendor can offer guidance and support, helping to elevate the company's capabilities through their expertise.

However, it's crucial to approach outsourcing with realistic expectations. Outsourced vendors are partners in development, not a panacea for internal deficiencies. Without a strong internal foundation, reliance on external entities can lead to a cycle of blame and missed expectations. It's often more challenging to manage outsourced relationships than in-house teams due to the additional layers of complexity such as communication barriers and cultural differences. The responsibility for a successful outcome lies not only with the vendor but also with the client's ability to manage and collaborate effectively. Hence, ensuring internal maturity is not just advisable but essential for the successful integration of outsourced services into a company's software development lifecycle.

R - Responsive Agile Culture

Once your company is able to reliably create valuable software, it's time to move onto the second baby step of Agile Outsourcing, building a responsive agile culture. This is almost certainly the most difficult step to take. Building a responsive agile culture has 3 pillars:

1. Equality
2. Trust
3. Flexibility
4. Investment

In the following sections we will dive into each of these areas as to how they relate to building a culture where outsourced projects have the highest chance of success.

Equality

The cultural value of equality plays a crucial role in the success of outsourced software development. This approach is centered around the philosophy that, despite the differences in employment status and geographic location, every individual is part of a single, unified team working towards a common objective. In effect, having one team, not many components that happen to be working together.

Creating such an inclusive team culture means that all members, whether full-time employees or outsourced contractors, are fully integrated into the company's processes and values. The concept goes beyond merely collaborating on tasks; it's about fostering a sense of shared identity and purpose. In this environment, team members are encouraged to contribute equally, share successes and failures, and hold collective responsibility for the project's outcome.

This unified team approach mitigates the 'us versus them' mindset that can often arise in outsourced arrangements. It encourages open communication, mutual respect, and genuine collaboration. As one team, members are expected to address challenges together, find solutions as a unit, and celebrate achievements as a collective. By eradicating the barriers that typically segregate employees from outsourced staff, companies can create a harmonious work culture that drives project success and aligns with the overall business strategy.

This model embraces mixed employment scrum teams, if you're using a scrum model of agile software development. This means that some members of the team may be employees, while others are from one, or even more, vendors. In the end, they are one team working towards one set of sprint goals. They are judged as a team, regardless of who pays their paycheck.

In this model, every team member's input is valued regardless of their contract type or vendor affiliation. This inclusivity not only boosts morale but also unleashes the full potential of a diverse workforce, harnessing a wide range of skills, experiences, and perspectives that enrich the development process and enhance the quality of the end product.

A successful method to help reiterate this approach is to give each scrum team, assuming you are using scrum teams, and name. It may have employees and contractors on the team, but from that point on is simply referred to by its name. This gives the team members a sense of identity and allows them to develop an inter-team culture.

The 'One Team' approach requires intentional effort from leadership to integrate and align all members. This might include joint training sessions, shared team-building activities, and consistent communication channels that ensure everyone is on the same page. By doing so, companies create a cohesive team dynamic that is essential for the long-term success of their outsourced software development initiatives.

The concept of equality across all members of a software development team, irrespective of their employment status, is a cornerstone of successful outsourcing. This means recognizing that titles and roles, such as that of an Architect, carry the same weight and responsibility whether the person is an in-house employee or an outsourced resource.

This approach to equality ensures that leadership roles and responsibilities are assigned based on merit, expertise, and talent, rather than on the basis of who signs the paycheck. It acknowledges that outsourced resources bring a wealth of knowledge and skills to the table, and it makes practical sense to utilize their full potential—both their technical abilities and their soft skills. After all, when a company outsources, it is not just purchasing a service; it is investing in the capabilities and expertise that the outsourced talent represents.

Moreover, this egalitarian approach enhances the team's resilience and flexibility. When each team member's contributions are valued equally, the team becomes more adaptive and better equipped to handle changes, such as scaling up or restructuring. This can be particularly beneficial when the time comes to expand the team or when there is a need to pivot quickly in response to market demands or project requirements.

By fostering a culture of equality, where outsourced professionals are fully integrated into the team, companies can maximize their investment. This not only boosts morale and encourages a sense of belonging among all team members but also contributes to a more dynamic and robust team capable of driving the project forward with greater innovation and efficiency.

Embracing the cultural value of 'Building One Team' can be an adjustment for internal employees who may consciously or unconsciously harbor a sense of superiority over outsourced talent. To transition to an egalitarian team culture, where outsourced members are seen as equals, several strategies can be implemented.

Leadership must pave the way by exemplifying the one-team ethos, treating all team members equally, whether they are in-house staff or outsourced partners. This equal treatment should be evident in all interactions and decisions, sending a clear message that the organization values all contributors the same.

Face-to-face interactions, whether virtual or physical, are invaluable in breaking down barriers. When team members have the opportunity to interact personally, stereotypes and misconceptions tend to dissolve, fostering mutual respect and understanding.

It's essential to communicate this cultural shift to outsourced resources as well. They should understand that their role is not to be subservient to in-house employees but to collaborate as equals to achieve common goals. Their input, expertise, and perspective are crucial to the team's success.

Resistance is to be expected, and some employees may need direct conversations to align with this new cultural value. It's important for management to address any reluctance or resistance head-on, ensuring all team members are on board with the new collaborative approach.

Transparency in communication is key. All team members should have access to the same product-related information, ensuring that no knowledge silos create a divide between 'us' and 'them'.

Successes and failures belong to the team as a whole. When accomplishments are celebrated, every contributing member, regardless of their employment status, should be acknowledged. Similarly, when challenges arise, they should be addressed collectively without assigning blame to a particular group.

Just as outsourced resources are often given cultural sensitivity training, internal employees should also be encouraged to learn about their colleagues' cultural backgrounds. This can range from understanding basic etiquette to recognizing significant cultural events and traditions, which helps in building a strong, unified team spirit.

By implementing these strategies, companies can ensure that their internal employees view and treat outsourced talent as equals, working together towards shared objectives and fostering a truly collaborative environment.

Integrating outsourced resources into an organization's existing software development structure can be a source of apprehension for internal employees. Concerns about job security and the perception of being replaced by lower-cost alternatives are common. Addressing these concerns requires a sensitive and strategic approach, rooted in the cultural value of equality and a clear communication of the organization's broader objectives.

First and foremost, it's crucial to reassure internal employees about their value and the security of their positions. This reassurance starts with a firm commitment from management to uphold the principle of equality across all team members, regardless of whether they are in-house employees or outsourced resources. Emphasizing that the addition of outsourced talent is not a cost-cutting measure to replace existing staff but a strategic decision to enhance the team's capabilities is key.

It's important to communicate the reasons behind outsourcing that extend beyond cost savings. These might include accessing specialized skills that complement the existing team, tapping into a global talent pool for diverse perspectives, or expanding the company's reach in different geographical markets. By framing outsourcing as a move towards building a more broadly sourced ecosystem, employees can understand the value it brings to the company as a whole.

Maintaining trust with internal employees is paramount. Any actions that contradict the message of equality, such as laying off internal staff in favor of outsourced workers, can irreparably damage trust and morale. Trust is built over time through consistent actions that align with the company's stated values and objectives. Management must be transparent and consistent in its actions and communications to foster a trusting environment.

Another essential aspect is to highlight and celebrate the unique contributions of internal employees. Recognizing their achievements, involving them in decision-making, and providing opportunities for growth and development can reinforce their value to the organization. This includes offering training and development opportunities that enable them to enhance their skills and stay competitive in the evolving tech landscape.

Finally, promoting a culture of collaboration and learning across the entire team can help internal employees see outsourced colleagues as partners in progress rather than threats to their job security. Encouraging knowledge sharing, joint problem-solving sessions, and team-building activities can foster a sense of unity and shared purpose.

In summary, reassuring internal resources when introducing outsourced talent requires a multi-faceted approach that emphasizes the value of all team members, upholds a culture of equality, and maintains transparency and trust. By clearly communicating the strategic reasons behind outsourcing and consistently demonstrating a commitment to all employees, organizations can create a harmonious and effective integrated development team.

Trust

In the realm of managing outsourced resources, two predominant styles are often observed. The first style, which can be referred to as the "Choke Hold," is characterized by tight control, critical oversight, and a predisposition towards punitive measures. Teams under this style of management often experience micro-management, with their actions scrutinized and creativity stifled, leading to a tense and unproductive work environment.

The second style, founded on "Trust," stands in stark contrast. Here, outsourced resources are regarded as equal partners, afforded the same respect and opportunities as in-house team members. This style is about nurturing a culture of mutual respect, continuous appreciation, and meaningful engagement in the creative process. It empowers teams to self-organize, fosters autonomy in decision-making, and encourages collaborative problem-solving without the burden of excessive hierarchical approvals.

This book advocates unequivocally for the trust-based approach to managing outsourced teams. While the choke hold approach may be more prevalent, it is the trust-based model that aligns with the principles of Agile Outsourcing and is essential for realizing the benefits outlined in this book. Embracing a management style that is grounded in trust can yield substantial benefits, such as heightened productivity, lower turnover rates, and a surge in innovation. It also leads to improved quality of deliverables and a reduction in risk.

Moreover, the trust-based management approach resonates with the fundamental human need for respect and recognition. When people feel valued and trusted, they are more likely to be engaged, take ownership of their work, and go above and beyond to contribute to the project's success. Thus, by adopting a trust-based management style, organizations not only foster a positive and empowering work environment but also set the stage for a more dynamic and effective partnership with their outsourced talent.

Flexibility

Embracing flexibility as a cultural value in software development outsourcing is a multifaceted approach, essential for harmonizing diverse global teams. This flexibility extends to an understanding and acceptance of varying cultural norms and traditions. Each culture brings its unique perspective, influencing problem-solving approaches and creativity, enriching the collaborative environment.

Acknowledging different holiday schedules is also crucial. It requires an adjustment in expectations and planning, respecting each region's customs and practices. This understanding fosters a respectful and inclusive workplace, even if it challenges certain ingrained attitudes towards work and leisure, as commonly seen in American work culture.

Moreover, flexibility involves being open to different frameworks and methodologies. It's about recognizing that there isn't a one-size-fits-all solution in technology and that different teams might have preferred tools and approaches that are equally effective.

Adapting to different working hours is another critical aspect, especially when collaborating across time zones. It means finding a balance that respects the personal lives of team members while ensuring project continuity.

Finally, flexibility in views on authority is crucial. Different cultures have varying perceptions of hierarchy and decision-making. In some cultures, authority is challenged and debated openly, while in others, it is accepted without question. Navigating these differences requires sensitivity and adaptability, ensuring that all team members, regardless of their cultural background, feel valued and heard.

In summary, the cultural value of flexibility in outsourcing is about creating an environment that respects and embraces diversity in all its forms, leading to a more dynamic, innovative, and effective software development process.

Fostering empathy in a software development team, particularly when working with outsourced members, is essential for creating a cohesive and productive environment. One effective way to develop this empathy is by taking the time to genuinely get to know your outsourced teammates beyond the scope of work. Understanding their interests, family life, professional ambitions, and hobbies can significantly bridge the gap often felt in remote collaborations.

Showing a genuine interest in them as individuals, not just as contributors to a project, is key. This can involve simple gestures like asking about their weekend plans, celebrating their personal milestones, or showing curiosity about their culture and traditions. Such interactions not only foster a more amicable work atmosphere but also pave the way for better understanding and patience when navigating the complexities of a diverse team.

Creating opportunities for informal interactions, whether through virtual coffee breaks or casual catch-up sessions, can help team members connect on a personal level. It's about seeing each other as people first and colleagues second. This approach nurtures empathy, leading to a more respectful and understanding work environment, where team members are more inclined to support and collaborate effectively with one another.

Ultimately, becoming more empathetic towards outsourced teammates is about building relationships based on mutual respect and understanding. It enhances team dynamics, improves communication, and contributes to a more inclusive and productive working environment.

Investment

The final cultural trait is based on mutual investment. This means that you as the outsourcing client invests in the individuals on your team, and they invest in you and your product.

Investing in outsourced resources and fostering their investment in the product they are building is a cornerstone of successful outsourcing relationships. Key to this is cultivating a sense of ownership among the outsourced team, making them view the product not merely as a task to be completed, but as 'their baby' — something they are passionately involved in and committed to nurturing.

Creating this environment of ownership involves more than just delegating tasks; it's about integrating the outsourced team into the fabric of the product's lifecycle. This can be achieved by actively involving them in various stages of the product development, from planning to execution to feedback analysis. Regularly sharing customer feedback, success stories, and words of appreciation from management with the outsourced team can significantly boost their sense of belonging and commitment to the product.

Furthermore, celebrating the product's milestones and successes as a joint achievement can reinforce their feeling of being a crucial part of the company's journey. It is also essential to provide them with opportunities to contribute ideas and feedback, making them feel heard and valued. By doing so, outsourced teams are more likely to take pride in their work, striving not just for completion but for excellence.

In turn, when outsourced teams see their contributions directly impacting the product's success and the company's growth, it creates a virtuous cycle. They become more motivated, innovative, and engaged, leading to higher quality outputs and a more successful product. This sense of ownership and pride in their work is key to transforming an outsourced team from a mere service provider to a vital part of your company's ecosystem.

Investing in the individuals who make up your outsourced team is a critical step in building a robust and effective partnership. This investment goes beyond the immediate needs of the project; it's about nurturing their professional growth, enhancing their skills, and expanding their understanding of not just the product, but also the market dynamics and the overarching vision of your company.

Encouraging continuous learning and professional development among your outsourced team members is key. Provide opportunities for them to acquire new technical skills, understand emerging market trends, and develop a deeper insight into the product's impact. This could involve access to training programs, workshops, mentoring, and even cross-functional involvement within the project.

Empowering team members with increasing responsibilities is another crucial aspect. Assign them roles that challenge their abilities and push them to innovate. This not only helps in their professional growth but also instills a deeper sense of ownership and commitment towards the project.

Understanding and catering to their career aspirations can further cement their loyalty and dedication. Regular discussions about their career goals, providing feedback, and recognizing their achievements can make a significant difference. Show them that their growth aligns with the company's success, making them a valuable asset to the organization.

Investing in individual team members should be viewed as a long-term strategy. The goal is to build a team that is not only skilled and knowledgeable but also deeply invested in the success of your product and company. By focusing on their personal and professional growth, you're not only enhancing their ability to contribute more effectively but also building a stronger, more committed team that will yield long-term benefits for your outsourcing endeavors.

Survey to Ensure Preparedness

Implementing a cultural transition that fosters equality, trust, flexibility, and investment between employees, leadership, and outsourced resources is a complex and ongoing process. To gauge the effectiveness of these efforts, organizations can deploy an anonymous survey. This survey serves as a barometer for the current state of the organizational culture and helps identify areas needing improvement.

Empowerment Survey Questions

1. Do you feel empowered to control your workload (the amount of work you are expected to do)?
   a. Yes, I feel empowered
   b. No, I do not feel empowered
2. Do you feel empowered to do your work the right way?
   a. Yes, I feel empowered
   b. No, I do not feel empowered

3. Do you feel empowered to make decisions regarding the tools and methods used to accomplish work?
    a. Yes, I feel empowered
    b. No, I do not feel empowered
4. Do you feel respected by the following team members?
    a. Product Owners and Product Managers
    b. Team Lead
    c. My Manager
    d. Management
    e. My Teammates
5. How well do members of your team share responsibility for the work assigned?
    a. Extremely Well
    b. Very Well
    c. Somewhat Well
    d. Not So Well
    e. Not Well
6. Do you feel micromanaged by any of the following roles?
    a. Product Owners and Product Managers
    b. Team Lead
    c. My Manager
    d. Management
    e. Other teammates
    f. Anyone else

How to Collect and Analyze the Results

In order to glean meaningful insights from the survey, it is crucial to ensure widespread participation across the team, employees and outsourced resources. Achieving near-total participation is a key success factor. To facilitate this, it is essential that the surveys are designed to be anonymous, guaranteeing that the responses of individual team members remain confidential and cannot be viewed by others.

For organizations with a diverse structure, especially those with different management styles or processes, it's advisable to categorize these segments distinctly when disseminating the survey. The purpose of this segmentation is not to judge or penalize any specific manager or team. Rather, it's to discern which groups are adequately prepared for outsourcing and which ones might need to focus on internal development first.

Regarding the distribution of the survey, a variety of tools are available. Organizations can effectively use integrated form tools within their existing O365 or Google Workspace subscriptions. Alternatively, dedicated survey platforms like Survey Monkey can be employed for this purpose.

It is also important to effectively communicate about the survey within your organization. Announcing its rollout, setting a clear deadline for completion, and sending timely reminders are all practices that help boost participation rates.

After collecting and analyzing the survey results, the next step is to interpret these insights to assess your organization's readiness for outsourcing. This involves evaluating the 'scores' or responses to each question in the context of your organization's specific environment and objectives. This evaluation will serve as a guide to whether your team is primed for outsourcing or if there are areas that require further internal development and alignment.

Preferred Responses

The following table outlines the preferred responses to the survey.

Question	Preferred Response
1	A: Employees and outsourced resources should feel totally empowered to control their workload. The pressure to do more should come from inter-team pressures and not external pressures. The teams should be striving to be the best they can be.
2	A: Employees and outsourced resources should feel totally empowered to make the decisions necessary to make the best product using the best process.
3	A: Employees and outsourced resources should feel totally empowered on the "how" to do their work.
4	All: Each individual should feel respected by all of the members of their team and the stakeholders in the team.
5	A: This is an indicator of the team's ability to self-organize and should be the highest level for the most optimized team performance.
6	None: We want to avoid micromanagement at all levels to ensure each individual can be their most effective

What to do if you scored poorly?

If the survey results indicate that your team is not aligning well with the preferred responses, indicating a lack of readiness for successful outsourcing, it's time to take a proactive approach. This situation calls for a two-pronged strategy. First, you can commence outsourcing with the segments of your organization that demonstrate readiness. These groups show alignment with the core values and readiness metrics necessary for effective outsourcing. Leveraging their strengths can set a positive example and provide learnings for the rest of the organization.

For the groups that did not fare well in the survey, focus on internal development and improvement. This involves engaging in open, transparent, and candid discussions with both team members and leaders. The objective of these discussions should be to identify the root causes of the misalignment and to collaboratively develop strategies to address these issues. It's crucial to create an environment where feedback is welcomed and acted upon, reinforcing the principle of continuous improvement.

Remember, the goal isn't to penalize teams for their current state but to identify areas for growth and to work collectively towards enhancing readiness for outsourcing. This approach helps in building a stronger foundation, ensuring that when these teams are eventually ready to embrace outsourcing, they do so with the necessary capabilities and mindset to succeed.

Creating An Agile Software Culture Summary

In summarizing the "Creating a Responsive Agile Culture" section for our book on agile outsourcing, we have delved deeply into four fundamental values crucial for the success of any agile outsourcing venture: Equality, Trust, Flexibility, and Investment.

At the heart of a responsive agile culture is the belief in and practice of equality. This value underscores the importance of viewing and treating every team member with equal respect and consideration, regardless of whether they are in-house employees or outsourced partners. Emphasizing equality fosters a sense of belonging and unity, essential for collaborative and efficient teamwork.

Trust is the cornerstone of any successful relationship, and in the context of agile outsourcing, it's indispensable. Cultivating an environment of trust involves not just believing in the capabilities of outsourced teams but also in their decision-making and problem-solving skills. Trust encourages autonomy and empowers teams to take ownership of their work, leading to more innovative and effective solutions.

The value of flexibility is particularly significant in a global outsourcing context. It encompasses being adaptable to various cultural norms, working hours, and differing approaches to problem-solving. Flexibility in working practices and mindsets is crucial for navigating the complexities of a diverse global workforce and ensures smoother integration and collaboration among team members from different backgrounds.

Finally, investment refers to the commitment to not only invest in the project but also in the people involved in it. This means nurturing the growth and development of each team member, ensuring they have opportunities to learn, evolve, and contribute meaningfully. Investment in people leads to a more engaged, skilled, and motivated workforce, ultimately driving the success of the outsourced project.

By weaving these values into the fabric of an organization's culture, businesses can create a more responsive, agile, and effective environment. This culture not only enhances the success of outsourcing endeavors but also contributes to the overall growth and evolution of the organization.

A - Adopt Agile Processes

Only after you've established a healthy culture and sense of ownership can you think about the process. A process that scales beyond the borders of your company and country. One that allows teams to be added to meet demand, quickly pivot to meet customers' needs, and provides the information customer success, marketing, and sales teams need to acquire and retain new customers.

General Purpose Processors

A new outsourcing model calls for a new framework for managing teams. In the following section we explore a novel framework, which is termed "General Product Processor," (GPP) inspired by the modular design of computer motherboards.

In this proposed paradigm, the primary unit of software delivery shifts from the individual to the team. Each team, composed typically of around five developers and one Software Development Engineer in Test (SDET) or Software Engineer in Test (SEIT), is equipped with a blend of junior and senior talents, including an architect. The SDET or SEIT plays a crucial role, focusing on automated testing, akin to a test engineer.

For the majority of companies developing B2B or B2C SaaS or mobile applications, the core teams should be the teams that can work on the majority of the application. Analogous to the cores in a CPU from Intel or AMD, these teams are versatile, capable of working on various aspects of the application. Nearly any request from product management could be worked by any of the teams. Just like adding more cores increases a CPU's capacity, adding more General Product Processors enhances the development capacity for standard application features.

In some scenarios, there's a need for specialized teams, akin to the cores in a Graphics Processing Unit (GPU) found on your NVIDIA graphics card. These teams, focusing on areas like AI, Big Data, and

Machine Learning, employ distinct techniques and tools compared to general features teams. Though more specialized, these 'GPU' teams remain relatively interchangeable within their specialization.

In rare instances, teams akin to Application-Specific Integrated Circuits (ASICs) might be necessary. These teams, highly specialized and unique, are used for tasks that require converting software functionalities into hardware for performance gains. An example would be a team dedicated to quantum encryption. While this may be a larger team today, it's very specialized given the state of the art. These teams, mirroring ASICs in their uniqueness and specialization, are costly and challenging to maintain.

In this analogy, product managers play the role of RAM. They distribute tasks to the various teams (cores) and consolidate the outcomes into a cohesive solution for the end-user similar to the computer program the different GPP teams need to process. They must then bring all of the components together into a package that customers desire. Communication between the teams and the product managers is facilitated by the 'buses' of the motherboard, paralleling the software development life cycle processes in an organization. This model emphasizes a team-centric approach, promoting scalability, flexibility, and maintainability in software development.

Benefits of This Model

The General Product Processor model offers a multitude of benefits, key among them being enhanced responsiveness and flexibility in meeting customer demands. By adopting this approach, companies gain the agility to redistribute resources swiftly and efficiently, ensuring that development capacity is allocated where it is most needed. This adaptability is particularly beneficial when prioritizing crucial features, allowing for a more dynamic and responsive development process.

A key benefit of the General Product Processor (GPP) framework is its scalability, enabling companies to grow beyond just a few teams while maintaining a sharp focus on their customers' highest priority requests. This scalability is achieved through the framework's modular design, which mirrors the components of a motherboard, allowing for the addition of new teams (akin to adding more processor cores) without disrupting the existing structure. Each team, whether functioning as a CPU, GPU, or ASIC unit, possesses a distinct yet flexible skill set, making it possible to swiftly reallocate resources and attention to areas of immediate customer need. This dynamic resource allocation ensures that as a company expands, it doesn't lose sight of customer-centric development. The prioritization of customer requests remains at the forefront, as the GPP framework promotes an agile and responsive environment where changing customer needs can be quickly addressed, regardless of the organization's size. This feature of the GPP framework is especially beneficial in today's rapidly evolving market, where the ability to adapt quickly to customer feedback and changing demands is a critical factor for success.

Another significant advantage of this model is its contribution to organizational resilience. In traditional setups, the departure of a key individual can jeopardize project continuity and stability. However, in a team-centric environment, reliance on any single individual is drastically reduced. This not only mitigates the risk associated with personnel changes but also fosters a more robust and sustainable development ecosystem.

Additionally, this approach addresses internal dynamics and team morale. In many development environments, there is a tendency for certain projects or features to be perceived as more prestigious or engaging, leading to envy or dissatisfaction among team members. The GPP model democratizes the distribution of both exciting and routine tasks, offering every team opportunities to engage in diverse projects. This equitable distribution of work helps in maintaining a balanced and motivated workforce.

Expanding on the versatility afforded by the General Product Processor framework, a significant benefit lies in its compatibility with modern, comprehensive frameworks. When the product architecture leverages such frameworks effectively, it allows for a remarkable fluidity in team roles and responsibilities. For instance, a JavaScript developer, traditionally confined to front-end tasks, can now seamlessly transition across various domains of the project. This includes working on back-end development, managing No-SQL databases, and even configuring Continuous Integration/Continuous Deployment (CI/CD) processes. This holistic approach not only maximizes the utility of each team member but also fosters a deeper understanding of the product as a whole. Consequently, this versatility leads to a more cohesive development process, as team members are not just isolated to one aspect of the project but are equipped and empowered to contribute across different technical fronts, enhancing both the efficiency and the quality of the software product. Such cross-functional capability is vital in today's fast-paced and ever-evolving tech landscape, where adaptability and comprehensive skill sets are key drivers of success. The GPP framework, therefore, not only optimizes resource utilization but also cultivates a workforce that is agile, knowledgeable, and highly capable in various aspects of software development.

Furthermore, this model cultivates larger, more collaborative communities within the organization. When challenges arise, having a broader pool of expertise and perspectives to draw upon can significantly expedite problem-solving and innovation. This communal approach to tackling issues not only enhances efficiency but also fosters a culture of collective responsibility and shared success. In sum, the GPP model presents a strategic shift towards a more resilient, equitable, and collaborative software development paradigm, aligning closely with contemporary needs and values in the tech industry.

Building Team Cores

For the successful implementation of GPPs, several critical factors must be addressed:

Standardization of Processes and Tools: The cornerstone of this methodology is the standardization of processes across all teams. It is essential that every team member is proficient in the same programming languages, utilizes the same set of tools, and follows a uniform Continuous Integration/Continuous Deployment (CI/CD) system. This uniformity ensures that any team can seamlessly pick up work from another, facilitating flexibility and efficiency.

Emphasis on Automation and Test Maintenance: Automation is a crucial component of this model. A robust suite of automated tests, integrated with an effective CI/CD pipeline, is vital. Equally important is the ongoing maintenance of these tests to ensure they remain effective and relevant. This approach reduces manual testing efforts and ensures consistent quality across the product.

Redistribution of Critical App Components: Perhaps the most challenging aspect is the reallocation of the most complex and critical parts of the application to different teams. While the original 'champion' of these components may still be available for consultation, the ownership must be transferred to ensure no single individual becomes a bottleneck. This transition may create initial resistance and power dynamic challenges but is crucial for fostering a resilient and adaptable team structure.

Rotational Exposure to Different Product Areas: To prevent teams from becoming pigeonholed into specific areas of the application, it's important to periodically rotate parts of the product among teams. This approach ensures that all teams gain exposure to various aspects of the application, enhancing their overall understanding and versatility.

Strategic Team Seeding and Knowledge Dissemination: When forming new teams, integrating members from existing teams is a strategic move. This seeding process helps in transferring the established culture, methodologies, and knowledge to the new team, promoting consistency and cohesion. Subsequently, backfilling the positions in the original teams with new members ensures continuous growth and fresh perspectives.

Balancing Specializations Within Teams: While some degree of specialization within teams is natural and beneficial – for instance, some teams may lean more towards UI development, while others may have a stronger back-end focus – it is important to maintain a balance. Teams should not become overly specialized in one area to the detriment of their overall capability. This balance ensures that each team remains versatile and capable of tackling a wide range of tasks within the application.

Prioritizing Well-Commented Code and Updated Documentation: An often underemphasized yet critical aspect of this model is the emphasis on well-commented code and regularly updated documentation, including architectural documents. In an environment where teams are interchangeable and work on various parts of the application, the clarity and accessibility of code become paramount. Well-commented code ensures that any team member, regardless of their prior exposure to a specific codebase, can understand the logic, purpose, and functionality of the code quickly and effectively.

In addition to code comments, maintaining up-to-date documentation is essential. This includes comprehensive architectural documents that outline the overall design, structure, and interaction of various components within the application. Such documentation serves as a guide and reference point for all teams, facilitating a deeper understanding of the broader system beyond the individual code snippets they work on. It also aids in onboarding new team members and serves as a valuable resource for planning future enhancements and troubleshooting existing issues.

Managing Teams: From an HR management perspective, these teams will need to be managed by somebody. "It's often useful to have one to two teams report to a software development manager, and all CPU, GPU or ASIC teams roll up to a director level role, but this will vary based on your organization.

Managing Knowledge Transfer: Effective knowledge transfer is a cornerstone of the GPP framework. It can be managed through regular inter-team workshops and documentation reviews, ensuring that knowledge is not siloed within a single team. Regularly scheduled 'knowledge-sharing sessions' where teams present their work and challenges to other teams can foster a culture of continuous learning. Additionally, maintaining comprehensive, up-to-date documentation and making it accessible to all teams helps in smoothing the knowledge transfer process.

Measuring Individual Performance: While team success is paramount, recognizing individual contributions is essential for morale and career progression. Managers should establish metrics that reflect both team achievements and individual contributions. Regular one-on-one meetings can be used to understand and acknowledge each team member's role in the team's success. Additionally, implementing a peer review system can provide insights into individual performance from a team perspective. This balanced approach ensures that while team performance is prioritized, individual efforts and talents are also recognized and nurtured.

Conflict Resolution: In a collaborative environment, conflicts are inevitable. Effective conflict resolution in the GPP framework involves fostering open communication and encouraging teams to address conflicts directly and constructively. Mediation sessions, led by a neutral party or manager, can be effective in resolving inter-team conflicts. Additionally, training teams in conflict resolution and communication skills can preempt many conflicts by providing team members with the tools to manage disagreements proactively and positively.

Addressing Scalability Limits: The scalability of the GPP framework is intrinsically tied to the maturity of the company's product management function. As organizations grow, the structure should evolve to support increased complexity. This might include dividing larger teams into smaller, more focused units or introducing additional layers of coordination for synchronization across teams. Regular assessments of team structures and workflows can identify bottlenecks or inefficiencies, guiding necessary adjustments. The key is to maintain the balance between flexibility and control, ensuring that teams remain agile and cohesive as the organization grows.

Implementing these strategies will not only facilitate a smoother transition to the Modular Mainframe Methodology but also ensure its long-term success and sustainability.

Interviewing for Team-Centric Engineering Roles: Strategies and Tips

When recruiting engineers for a setting where the team's efficacy outweighs individual glory, the interview process should be meticulously designed to identify candidates who not only excel technically but also thrive in collaborative environments. Here are key strategies and tips for conducting effective interviews:

Assessing Collaborative Skills: Inquire about the candidate's past experiences working in teams. Encourage them to share specific instances where they contributed to a team's success, overcame a team-based challenge, or played a pivotal role in a collaborative project. This not only sheds light on their teamwork skills but also on their ability to navigate the complexities of group dynamics.

Understanding the Approach to Problem Solving: Pose situational or hypothetical problems that require a collaborative approach to solve. Observe not just the technical solution provided but also how the candidate incorporates team interaction in their problem-solving process. This will reveal their ability to think in terms of team dynamics and collective problem-solving.

Evaluating Communication Skills: Effective communication is crucial in a team-centric environment. Assess the candidate's ability to articulate complex ideas clearly and their capacity to listen and understand others' perspectives. Role-playing exercises, where candidates have to explain technical concepts to a non-technical person, can be particularly revealing.

Valuing Diversity and Inclusivity: Explore their attitude towards diversity and inclusivity. Understanding and valuing diverse perspectives is key in a collaborative environment. Ask how they have adapted to work effectively with diverse teams or how they address different viewpoints.

Probing for Learning and Adaptability: In a dynamic team environment, the willingness to learn from others and adapt is vital. Discuss how they have adapted to new technologies or methodologies based on team requirements or feedback. This assesses their flexibility and eagerness to grow within a team setting.

Scenarios on Feedback and Critique: Present scenarios that involve giving and receiving constructive feedback. This can illustrate how the candidate deals with feedback, both as a giver and a receiver, and their ability to maintain a positive and constructive team atmosphere.

Checking References with a Team Focus: When conducting reference checks, focus on obtaining insights about the candidate's ability to work in team settings. Ask previous employers or colleagues about the candidate's role in team projects and their impact on the team's overall performance and morale.

Cultural Fit Assessment: Ensure the candidate aligns with the organization's culture, especially the aspects that emphasize teamwork and collaboration. Discuss the company's values and observe how the candidate resonates with them.

By focusing on these areas during the interview process, you can more effectively identify candidates who are not only technically proficient but also possess the collaborative spirit, communication skills, and adaptability necessary to thrive in a team-centric engineering environment.

GPP Augmenting Agile

The General Product Processor (GPP) framework, while embodying core principles of agility and flexibility akin to traditional Agile methodologies, distinguishes itself in several key aspects:

Holistic Team Versatility vs. Role-Specific Teams: Traditional Agile development often relies on role-specific team members - such as dedicated front-end developers, back-end developers, and database managers. In contrast, the GPP framework emphasizes holistic team versatility. It encourages members to acquire a broader skill set. This approach not only ensures team adaptability but also fosters a deeper understanding and ownership of the product among all team members.

Modular Team Structure Inspired by Motherboard Design: The GPP framework introduces a unique analogy by comparing team structures to the components of a computer motherboard, such as CPUs, GPUs, and ASICs. This modular approach contrasts with traditional Agile teams, which are typically not modeled after such a distinct hardware-inspired paradigm. The GPP framework's modular design provides a clear, organized way to structure teams based on their function and specialization, enhancing scalability and flexibility in resource allocation.

Emphasis on Cross-Functional Interchangeability: Unlike traditional Agile, where teams might be siloed based on their project or component of work, the GPP framework emphasizes interchangeable and cross-functional teams. This interchangeability ensures that teams can dynamically shift their focus and resources as required, akin to how various processor cores in a CPU can handle different tasks. This aspect of the GPP framework is particularly beneficial in managing complex and large-scale projects, ensuring smooth transitions and continuity despite fluctuating project demands.

Enhanced Focus on Automation and Continuous Learning: While traditional Agile methodologies do emphasize continuous improvement, the GPP framework places a stronger emphasis on automation and test maintenance, integral to its operational philosophy. This focus on automation, especially in testing and deployment, aligns with the GPP's goal of maximizing efficiency and reducing manual effort, allowing teams to focus more on innovation and problem-solving.

Strategic Team Seeding for Knowledge Dissemination: The GPP framework proposes a unique approach to team formation and knowledge transfer, advocating for the strategic seeding of new teams with members from existing teams. This approach, which is less emphasized in traditional Agile practices, ensures a consistent transfer of knowledge, culture, and methodologies across teams, thereby fostering a more integrated and cohesive development environment.

In summary, while the GPP framework shares Agile's core principles of flexibility and iterative development, it introduces novel concepts such as a hardware-inspired team structure, cross-functional versatility, and strategic team seeding. These elements collectively contribute to a more adaptive, efficient, and cohesive software development process, particularly suited for large-scale and complex projects.

General Product Processors Enables SAFe and LeSS

The GPP framework can be a potent enhancer for the Scaled Agile Framework (SAFe) and Large-Scale Scrum (LeSS) in larger organizations, thanks to its unique approach to team structure and project management. In the context of SAFe, which aims to scale Agile practices across an enterprise, GPP's emphasis on interchangeable, modular teams aligns seamlessly. This modularity facilitates the scaling of Agile practices by allowing teams to be easily reconfigured or expanded without disrupting the overall workflow. It also facilitates a smoother Agile Release Train (ART) process, a core component of SAFe, by ensuring that each 'train' or team is capable of handling various aspects of a project, thereby promoting cross-functional collaboration and reducing dependencies.

Similarly, in the realm of LeSS, which is focused on scaling Scrum in large-scale software development, GPP's approach can be highly beneficial. By advocating for well-structured, balanced teams with a mix of skills and specializations, GPP ensures that each Scrum team is self-sufficient and versatile. This complements the LeSS principle of creating feature-centric teams rather than component-centric ones, enhancing the framework's overall efficiency. Moreover, GPP's emphasis on standardized processes, automation, and documentation aligns with the LeSS guidelines of simplicity and transparency, further streamlining the Scrum process at scale.

In both SAFe and LeSS, GPP's insistence on flexible, yet structured team dynamics, coupled with its focus on shared knowledge and continuous learning, can help large organizations overcome common challenges associated with scaling Agile methodologies. These include issues related to coordination, integration, and maintaining a consistent Agile culture across multiple teams. By integrating GPP's principles, companies can foster a more cohesive and adaptable Agile environment, leading to more successful implementation of either SAFe or LeSS in larger corporate settings.

A Framework for Mid-Sized to Enterprise Scale Companies

The GPP framework is particularly suited for medium to large-sized companies due to its structural and resource requirements. For smaller companies with only one or two Scrum teams, the luxury of implementing this model may not be feasible. This is largely because the framework hinges on the ability to create multiple, specialized yet interchangeable teams that can flexibly shift focus and resources as needed. Smaller companies often lack the sheer number of team members required to diversify and rotate effectively within such a structure.

However, as these smaller companies grow and scale, the GPP framework offers a robust guideline for organizational design. It provides a blueprint for expanding their software development operations in a manner that balances specialization with versatility, ensuring that no single team or individual becomes a bottleneck. This model encourages a sustainable scaling strategy, where new teams can be integrated seamlessly, and knowledge and culture are disseminated effectively through strategic team member rotation.

For startups and small enterprises, understanding the principles of the GPP framework can be beneficial. As they expand, they can gradually adopt aspects of this model, transitioning from a more centralized team structure to a more modular and scalable approach. This forward-thinking strategy not only prepares them for future growth but also instills a culture of collaboration and adaptability from the outset, setting a strong foundation for long-term success in the dynamic landscape of software development.

Conclusion

The GPP framework, inspired by the modular and interconnected design of computer motherboards, presents a transformative approach to software development. It challenges the traditional emphasis on individual 'rock-star' developers and shifts the focus to collaborative, versatile teams - akin to the CPU, GPU, and ASIC units on a motherboard. This paradigm not only democratizes the development process but also enhances organizational resilience, agility, and innovation.

As with any motherboard, the key to this framework's success lies in its interconnectedness and harmony among its components. The teams, functioning like various processor cores, bring their unique strengths yet remain adaptable and interchangeable, fostering a dynamic environment where collective success trumps individual accolades. Product managers, akin to the RAM, orchestrate these teams, ensuring that tasks are distributed effectively and that the final product is a cohesive and well-integrated solution.

Implementing the GPP framework necessitates careful planning and management, particularly in terms of knowledge transfer, conflict resolution, and scalability. It requires a cultural shift towards valuing team achievements, balancing individual specializations, and ensuring continuous learning and adaptability. For medium to large-sized companies, this framework provides a scalable, flexible, and robust model for growth and innovation, allowing them to thrive in the ever-evolving landscape of software development.

In conclusion, the General Product Processor framework is more than just a method for software development; it's a blueprint for building a future where teams are the cornerstone of creativity and efficiency, mirroring the intricate yet harmonious workings of a well-designed motherboard. It's a vision for an environment where collaboration, shared knowledge, and flexibility drive the journey towards technological advancement and organizational success.

SDLC

Once the teams are organized you can turn your attention to the software development lifecycle (SDLC). There are several frameworks used to implement agile including SCRUM, SAFe, LeSS, XP, and so on. In the following section we will focus on common elements that can be included in any of the major frameworks.

Document Your SDLC

The documentation of the Software Development Life Cycle (SDLC) is a crucial element in agile outsourcing, serving as a comprehensive guide for the entire process of software development, from conception to deployment and maintenance. This documentation stands as a clear and precise roadmap, delineating the methodologies and practices employed in building, testing, deploying, and improving software. Its significance is particularly profound for the seamless integration and consistent functioning of both in-house and outsourced teams, ensuring that everyone is on the same page regarding expectations and procedures.

Moreover, a well-documented SDLC proves to be an invaluable asset in training and onboarding new team members, including those from outsourced partners. It allows for an efficient and effective induction process, enabling new members to quickly grasp the established procedures and standards. The dynamic nature of technology and methodologies necessitates regular updates to the SDLC documentation. This ensures that the processes remain relevant and effective in the face of evolving technologies and changing business objectives. Importantly, incorporating feedback from teams into the SDLC fosters a culture of continuous improvement, enabling refinements and enhancements based on real-world experiences and challenges encountered by the team.

Furthermore, the documentation of the SDLC is not merely a set of instructions; it represents a vital element for compliance with various frameworks and is crucial during technical due diligence processes such as acquisitions. It demonstrates to auditors and potential acquirers the robustness, standardization, and repeatability of the software development practices. In essence, a well-maintained SDLC documentation reflects the maturity and professionalism of the software development practice, making it a foundational component that underpins growth, learning, compliance, and business readiness.

Feature Management Process

Road mapping serves as a strategic blueprint, guiding product management and development teams in aligning on significant feature releases. Essential to the development process, it acts as a navigational chart for the project, setting out the major enhancements and innovations planned for the product. To foster a truly collaborative environment, this roadmap must be an open document to all involved parties, including outsourced members, ensuring their insights and suggestions are valued and considered.

Keeping the roadmap current and sharing updates regularly is vital for maintaining clarity and focus. It keeps everyone on the same page and allows teams to adjust to shifts in market demands or strategic direction. Moreover, alongside this proactive planning, there must be a responsive system in place for unexpected demands. A clearly defined and well-communicated process for addressing urgent customer needs, bugs, or critical feedback ensures that such issues are handled efficiently without derailing ongoing projects.

The integration of feedback and the flexibility to adapt to emerging requirements not only catalyze innovation but also foster a deep sense of trust and ownership across the team. By involving all team members in the road mapping process and valuing their contributions, organizations can cultivate a culture where outsourced and in-house teams work seamlessly together, driving the product towards success.

Requirement Management Process

Creating well-structured user stories or product requirement documents (PRDs) is vital in software development, especially when managing outsourced teams. These documents should utilize simple and direct language to convey the essence of the requirements, incorporating mock-ups and context wherever possible to provide visual aids and a deeper understanding of the expected outcomes. Each story or PRD should clearly articulate the 'who', 'what', 'why', and 'when' of a request, ensuring that the development team can grasp the user's needs, the functionality to be developed, its value proposition, and the timeline for delivery.

The INVEST model serves as an excellent guideline for shaping these stories or PRDs. According to this model, each user story should be Independent, allowing it to stand on its own without dependencies on other stories; Negotiable, so it can evolve and be refined until it's included in an iteration; Valuable, delivering clear benefit to the end user; Estimable, so the team can determine the effort required; Sized appropriately or Small, ensuring it's manageable and can be completed in a reasonable timeframe; and Testable, providing enough information for the development of test scenarios.

The process of grooming stories is a fundamental aspect of delivering high-quality software, as it ensures that the requirements presented to the development team are clear, concise, and actionable. Grooming, also known as backlog refinement, involves reviewing and revising user stories or product requirements to ensure they are well-defined and prioritized correctly. This process is crucial because it serves as the foundation for the development work that follows. When stories are properly groomed, they provide a clear and comprehensive understanding of what needs to be accomplished, thereby reducing ambiguities and the potential for misinterpretation. This clarity not only aids developers in understanding the scope and details of their tasks but also facilitates accurate estimations of effort and resources required. Moreover, well-groomed stories enable the development team to focus on delivering value to the customer by ensuring that each requirement directly aligns with the customer's needs and expectations. In essence, grooming stories is not just about organizing the work; it's about setting the stage for efficient and effective software development that consistently meets or exceeds customer expectations.

The clarity of these well-groomed requirements is crucial, as they often become the point of reference when there's a language barrier or when verbal communication might lead to misunderstandings. A good practice is to test the clarity of the stories by translating them into the developer's native language and back to English using tools like Google Translate. This can reveal any potential ambiguities or confusions in interpretation. This level of attention to detail in creating user stories or PRDs can greatly reduce miscommunication, streamline the development process, and enhance the quality of the software being developed, making them an indispensable tool in the agile outsourcing framework.

Customer Centricity Process

Instilling a customer-centric ethos in outsourced teams is crucial for aligning their efforts with your company's broader objectives. To achieve this, it's essential to bridge the gap between your customers and your outsourced resources. Far from keeping them in separate silos, it's beneficial to foster direct interactions where feasible. This direct exposure to customer feedback, inquiries, and needs provides invaluable context and understanding. It illuminates the 'why' behind the tasks they're executing, which can significantly enhance the quality and relevance of their work.

An essential component of making outsourced teams customer-centric is ensuring they are privy to customer feedback. Whether it's praise for a feature well-implemented or criticism for a missed mark, such feedback is a powerful motivator and educator. It deepens the outsourced team's sense of involvement and investment in the product, and in turn, encourages them to innovate and improve. Celebrating successes together reinforces a shared sense of achievement and fosters a more unified team spirit.

Moreover, empowering outsourced resources to act as ambassadors of your product to customers can be highly advantageous. Given their in-depth understanding of the product's technicalities, they can offer insights and solutions that might otherwise be overlooked. However, this empowerment comes with a responsibility. It's imperative that outsourced team members are well-versed in your company's values and communication guidelines. They must be equipped to represent your brand accurately and professionally, ensuring that every customer interaction reflects positively on your company.

In essence, making outsourced teams customer-centric isn't just about giving them tasks; it's about integrating them into the fabric of your company's relationship with its customers. This integration requires a strategic approach to communication, training, and empowerment, enabling these teams to contribute meaningfully to your company's customer-focused goals.

Ceremonies

Establishing a rhythm of regular ceremonies, adhering to a consistent schedule, is pivotal for agile teams, particularly when coordinating across multiple time zones. The cornerstone of these ceremonies is the daily scrum, a concise, focused gathering designed to synchronize the day's efforts. During this meeting, team members from product management to development discuss their recent work, outline their plans for the day, and seek assistance for any impediments they're encountering. Brevity is key here; a well-conducted scrum is a sprint, not a marathon, wrapping up within a 15-minute window. Participation isn't just encouraged; it's compulsory for the ceremony's success.

The specific ceremonies beyond the daily scrum may vary based on the chosen agile methodology, but typically include a grooming session to discuss upcoming work, sprint planning to assign and estimate effort, sprint review to demonstrate completed work, and a retrospective to identify improvements. These ceremonies create structure and provide regular touchpoints for the team to collaborate and reflect.

However, the agile framework isn't intended to congest calendars with meetings. Outside these structured ceremonies, encourage ad-hoc discussions and empower team members to collaborate as needed. The goal is to keep everyone's day clear for productive work, channeling most collaborative efforts into these dedicated agile ceremonies to maximize efficiency and focus.

Quality Process

In the era of agile outsourcing, the function of software testing must undergo a significant transformation, particularly when teams are scattered across different time zones. The traditional role of manual testers is rapidly evolving to meet the demands of continuous integration and delivery pipelines. As a result, we see a decisive shift towards automated testing, which necessitates the role of testers to expand into that of a Software Development Engineer in Test (SDET) or a Software Engineer in Test (SEIT).

The SDET is no longer merely a gatekeeper of quality at the end of a development cycle but is now integral to the development process from the onset. Their primary responsibility shifts from manual testing to creating comprehensive automated testing frameworks that allow developers to integrate quality assurance into their daily workflows. This approach enables the entire team to contribute to testing, with the SDET guiding and facilitating these efforts.

An SDET's role also encompasses being the steward of quality, ensuring that testing is not an afterthought but a continuous, integral part of the development lifecycle. They monitor and manage quality metrics, provide insights into quality trends, and hold the team accountable to agreed-upon quality standards. By empowering the team with tools and processes that facilitate automated testing, SDETs help build a culture of quality where everyone is responsible for the integrity and reliability of the software. Through this evolved role, SDETs contribute significantly to the overall efficiency and effectiveness of the team, ensuring that the software meets both functional and non-functional requirements consistently.

Since quality in software development is not a domain confined to a single role; it is a collective responsibility that spans across the entire team. A culture of quality begins with product management, which must define features and functions clearly and comprehensively to avoid ambiguities that can lead to bugs. Developers must then embody this vision, crafting code that not only functions but is robust and resilient. Similarly, Software Development Engineers in Test (SDET) or Software Engineers in Test (SEIT) are instrumental in creating the frameworks that empower every team member to take ownership of quality assurance.

This shared responsibility ensures that quality checks are woven into every stage of the development process. Unit testing validates the smallest parts of the application, integration testing ensures that these parts work together seamlessly, and UI layer testing confirms the end-user experience aligns with expectations. Beyond functionality, security and performance testing are critical to safeguard and streamline the application, while exploratory testing allows testers to go beyond predefined cases to uncover potential issues.

The quality process does not only include automated tests, it must also include code and security review processes. Tooling must be put in place for distributed and asynchronous code and security reviews and it must become the expectation that every element of code undergoes this process before being admitted to the master code repository.

When defects do arise, the response should be collective and collaborative. The discovery of a bug is not a moment to assign blame but an opportunity for the team to rally, diagnose, and rectify the issue together. By fostering a culture where quality is everyone's business, the team not only improves the product but also strengthens their unity and shared commitment to excellence.

The pivotal milestone in the quality assurance process is the role of product management as the gatekeeper for software features. They possess the crucial responsibility of validating each feature against the 'voice of the customer,' which they represent. This validation process is integral, as it ensures that what the development team delivers aligns precisely with customer expectations and requirements. The power vested in product management to accept or reject features acts as a critical checks-and-balances system, maintaining the integrity of the product and its alignment with customer needs.

Once a feature is accepted by product management, it transitions into the release management phase. However, the journey of quality assurance doesn't conclude here. The release management process is layered with numerous quality checks that persist until the software is successfully deployed in production. This phase encompasses a series of rigorous testing procedures, including deployment testing, which verifies the deployment process itself; further security testing, ensuring that the new features do not introduce vulnerabilities; and smoke testing, which quickly checks that the most critical functions of the software are working after deployment.

The emphasis during this phase is not only on the correctness of the feature but also on its performance in the production environment. It involves meticulous configuration to ensure the software operates optimally and efficiently in its live setting. This comprehensive approach to quality—from development through to production—ensures that each feature not only meets the functional requirements but also contributes to a stable, secure, and high-performing product. This end-to-end focus on quality is essential in delivering a product that not only satisfies customer needs but also enhances their overall experience with the software.

CI/CD Process

`In the landscape of modern software development, Continuous Integration/Continuous Deployment (CI/CD) systems are not just beneficial—they are indispensable, especially for distributed teams. The CI/CD pipeline acts as the technical backbone, ensuring that the collective efforts of dispersed teams converge seamlessly into a cohesive product. It's the embodiment of technical synergy that underpins the Synchronized Work approach, a pivotal concept in facilitating smooth and efficient remote collaborations. While entire books have been written on this process, we will review the main elements of a strong CI/CD pipeline that supports distributed teams.

The integration of version control, such as Git, into the CI/CD pipeline is foundational. It creates a solid framework for tracking changes, facilitating code reviews, and automating builds upon code merges. This level of integration is instrumental in preserving the integrity of the main branch and ensuring that any integration issues are identified at the earliest possible stage.

Automated builds are a cornerstone of CI/CD, enabling teams to compile code and execute unit tests automatically with each code check-in. This proactive measure is crucial in the early detection of integration mishaps, thus saving time and resources that would otherwise be spent on later-stage troubleshooting.

Test automation extends beyond unit testing to encompass integration and acceptance tests, forming a comprehensive net to catch bugs and regressions promptly. By automating this process, distributed teams can assure the quality of the software without the bottlenecks of manual testing.

The use of containerization tools, such as Docker, brings about environment consistency, effectively bridging the gap between development and production. This uniformity addresses the notorious "it works on my machine" syndrome, paving the way for smooth transitions through the various stages of deployment.

Deployment automation, complemented by structured approval gates, facilitates a steady flow of software delivery across environments. This systematic approach not only accelerates the deployment process but also integrates checks and balances to maintain quality standards.

The inclusion of rollback mechanisms provides a safety net, enabling teams to swiftly revert to a previous stable state in case of deployment hiccups. This feature is essential for maintaining service continuity and user trust.

Monitoring and logging tools integrated into the CI/CD pipeline provide real-time insights into application performance and offer diagnostic capabilities to rapidly address any operational issues.

Security scans within the pipeline are vital for early detection of vulnerabilities, embedding security into the very fabric of the development process and ensuring compliance with standards.

An artifact repository is a key component for managing build artifacts, which are essential for consistent and reliable deployments across all environments.

Infrastructure as Code (IaC) is a modern practice that ensures infrastructure changes are version-controlled and auditable, facilitating governance and compliance.

Configuration management and secret management tools help manage application configurations and sensitive data, keeping them secure and isolated from the codebase.

Lastly, integrating collaboration tools with the CI/CD pipeline keeps distributed teams aligned and informed about the status of the development process, fostering a culture of transparency and collective responsibility.

In sum, a robust CI/CD pipeline is the lifeblood of distributed teams, enabling them to deliver high-quality software with speed and precision, while also fostering a culture of continuous improvement and collaboration.

Release Process

The release process in a globally distributed software development setup is a multifaceted operation that demands meticulous planning, robust tooling, and a clear delineation of responsibilities. It is imperative that any member of the development team, irrespective of their geographical location, can initiate code deployments into lower-tier environments for preliminary smoke testing. This initial phase of testing is ideally managed through automated frameworks that can swiftly validate the functionality and stability of the software, thereby ensuring that any potential issues are flagged and addressed well before the production stage.

An essential aspect of this process is the democratization of deployment capabilities. Developers across the globe should be equipped with the tools and permissions necessary to deploy release candidates. This flexibility enables continuous integration and delivery workflows and allows for a more agile response to both planned updates and unforeseen production issues. By standardizing these tools and access protocols, organizations ensure that technical leaders in any time zone can autonomously manage emergency interventions without the inefficiency of waiting for colleagues in distant regions to start their workday.

However, such an open system necessitates rigorous compliance measures to safeguard sensitive product-level data. Access to production environments should be stringently controlled, granted only to a select group of trusted personnel—some of whom may be direct employees, others outsourced partners, depending on the compliance requirements. This privileged access should be under constant surveillance, with all interactions meticulously logged and subject to real-time monitoring to prevent any unauthorized activities. Additionally, every access instance should be backed by a compelling business justification, ensuring that the integrity of production data is never compromised.

In summary, the release process in a distributed development environment must strike a balance between agility and control. By empowering developers with the necessary tools for deployment and instituting rigorous compliance checks, organizations can maintain a rapid and responsive release cycle while upholding the highest standards of data security and regulatory compliance.

Support Process

When it comes to refining the support process for outsourced and geographically distributed teams, clarity and structure are paramount. The process must be meticulously mapped out, ensuring that standard bugs and issues are seamlessly integrated into the product management workflow and assigned a priority that aligns them with the work in upcoming sprints. This systematic approach ensures that bug resolution is balanced against new feature development and that the team's focus remains on delivering consistent value.

However, not all issues can be slotted into the regular sprint cycle—some require immediate attention. For such urgent matters, a clearly defined escalation procedure is vital. There are generally two approaches: one that taps into the existing sprint team's resources for critical fixes, and another that employs a dedicated Level 2 support team for handling such escalations. The use of a specialized Level 2 team should be judicious, activated only under stringent criteria to avoid disrupting the sprint's flow. These individuals, whether part of the internal staff or outsourced, must have quick access to relevant information, including production data when necessary, to address and resolve issues effectively.

Language barriers also need thoughtful consideration in this support framework. While there's no inherent obstacle to involving outsourced Level 2 support in direct customer interactions, it's crucial to moderate these exchanges. Unfiltered access is not advisable for safeguarding customer experience and ensuring clear communication. As such, a protocol should be in place for when and how Level 2 support engages with customers, always keeping customer interests at the forefront.

Lastly, fostering a strong rapport between Level 1 and Level 2 support teams is essential. They should not operate in silos but rather as an interconnected unit, with open lines of communication and mutual trust. This relationship is underpinned by regular interactions, knowledge sharing, and a supportive culture that recognizes the integral role each tier plays in overall customer satisfaction. By reinforcing these connections, support teams can operate more cohesively, ensuring quick, effective, and empathetic customer service that upholds the company's reputation and customer trust.

Roadblock Management Process

In the realm of software development, particularly when teams and resources are dispersed across various geographies and time zones, the proficiency in making roadblocks visible, effectively escalating them, and resolving them promptly is of paramount importance. The challenges posed by distance, cultural differences, and asynchronous communication can exacerbate these roadblocks, potentially causing delays and diminishing productivity. Hence, it's crucial to adopt strategies that ensure these impediments are swiftly and efficiently managed.

A pivotal aspect of this process is the establishment of a centralized tracking system. Such a system allows all team members to report and view the status of tasks, including any impediments, ensuring transparency and real-time updates. This could be facilitated through platforms like JIRA, Trello, or Asana. Complementing this, regular stand-up meetings or check-ins, scheduled at a convenient time for all involved time zones, encourage team members to discuss challenges openly. Additionally, implementing dashboard tools that provide a high-level view of the project and highlight bottlenecks can aid in quickly pinpointing areas needing immediate attention.

The escalation of roadblocks requires a clear, predefined protocol outlining the steps for reporting and escalating issues, including designated points of contact and expected response times. Appointing project managers or leads in each geographical location, who possess the authority to make decisions, ensures that issues can be escalated and addressed locally. Including representatives from different functional areas in each regional team fosters a diverse set of perspectives in problem-solving.

Forming rapid response teams equipped to mobilize quickly and address critical roadblocks is another crucial strategy. These teams, comprising members from different time zones, ensure round-the-clock problem-solving capabilities. Additionally, scheduling overlap hours for real-time collaboration across time zones facilitates focused problem-solving sessions. Empowering local teams to make decisions within a certain scope reduces delays caused by waiting for approvals from team members in different time zones.

Knowledge sharing sessions where common roadblocks and their resolutions are discussed build a repository of solutions for future reference. Moreover, embracing strong asynchronous communication practices, where necessary details about a roadblock and its context are clearly documented, allows team members in different time zones to contribute effectively.

To enhance these strategies, cultural sensitivity training is essential to help team members understand and respect different working styles and communication preferences. Leveraging collaboration tools like Slack, Microsoft Teams, or Zoom ensures continuous connectivity, regardless of location. Furthermore, a feedback mechanism where team members can suggest improvements to the process of handling roadblocks is vital for continuous process enhancement.

By implementing these integrated strategies, organizations can significantly improve their handling of roadblocks in distributed software development settings, leading to more efficient project execution and reduced turnaround times.

Tooling

Selecting the right tooling for software project management is a critical decision, especially when dealing with outsourced and geographically distributed teams. The market offers a variety of tools from providers like Atlassian, Wrike, Monday.com, and others, each with its own set of features and capabilities. The primary objective of these tools is to establish a central source of truth for the entire development process. This includes a comprehensive repository for what needs to be built, tracking defects, and understanding how each task, test, or user story integrates into the broader project scope.

However, it's not just about choosing the right tool; it's also about utilizing these tools effectively. Every element within the project management software should be meticulously documented and updated. This approach ensures that, at any given moment, team members can access all necessary information without the need for additional communication or clarification. Imagine a scenario where a critical team member is suddenly unavailable – in such cases, well-documented and updated tools can prevent project delays and confusion.

Furthermore, these tools should foster transparency and collaboration, allowing all team members, regardless of their location, to have an equal understanding and involvement in the project. This means having clear visibility into project timelines, dependencies, and progress. The right tool, when used to its full potential, not only streamlines the development process but also mitigates the risks associated with distributed teamwork, such as miscommunication and delays. Therefore, when selecting and implementing project management software, it's essential to prioritize ease of use, accessibility, and the ability to provide a comprehensive view of the project at any given time. This ensures that every team member, whether they are in-house or outsourced, has the necessary information to contribute effectively to the project's success.

Information Sharing

Incorporating agile methodologies into software development, especially in the context of outsourcing, demands a seamless integration of communication strategies across all teams and stakeholders. The collated details from both in-house and outsourced team members are pivotal in shaping the decisions and information flow within the organization. This necessitates a framework where all stakeholders, be it internal or external, have access to up-to-date and easily comprehensible channels that inform them about the ongoing progress, feature developments, and any identified defects.

For instance, the marketing department should have clear visibility on the schedule of marketing-related releases, enabling them to align their strategies and campaigns accordingly. The finance team needs to be kept in the loop about the progress against financial projections and budgets, ensuring fiscal alignment with the development roadmap. Similarly, executive management should have an overarching view of the project timelines, including any deviations or advancements, to ensure strategic alignment and informed decision-making.

The sales department plays a crucial role in managing customer expectations and hence should be updated regularly about the development queue, especially regarding features that are in high demand by clients. This level of transparency enables them to communicate effectively with clients, thus fostering trust and reliability.

While the need for total transparency with external stakeholders might not be as acute as it is internally, establishing a standard communication protocol is essential. Regular updates, progress reports, and insights into the development process can significantly enhance trust and confidence in the company's capabilities.

The key to making this ecosystem work efficiently lies in the uniformity of tools and processes used across both in-house and outsourced teams. It's essential to avoid creating silos of information or segregating teams based on their employment status. By ensuring that all teams, regardless of their geographical or organizational positioning, use the same tools and follow the same processes, the organization can effectively synchronize its development efforts. This unified approach is crucial for accurately translating the progress made by various teams into cohesive, comprehensive information that can be disseminated to all relevant stakeholders, thereby reinforcing the overarching goals of the agile outsourcing model.

Adopting an Agile Process Summary

As we conclude the Adopting Agile Processes section of our book, it's imperative to reflect on the three pivotal themes that form the bedrock of our approach to modern agile outsourcing.

At the heart of our discourse is the innovative GPP model, inspired by the intricate design of computer motherboards. This model revolutionizes team management by shifting the primary unit of software delivery from the individual to the team. Each team, akin to the cores in a CPU, is equipped with a diverse blend of talents, capable of tackling a wide array of tasks. This approach not only enhances the team's versatility and adaptability but also ensures that developmental efforts are evenly distributed, fostering an environment of shared responsibility and collective success. Specialized teams, analogous to GPU cores, bring their expertise to bear on complex areas like AI and Big Data, while ultra-specialized units, similar to ASICs, handle niche, high-performance tasks. The GPP model, therefore, offers a dynamic and flexible framework for managing teams, crucial for agile outsourcing in today's globalized software development landscape.

A cornerstone of our approach is the seamless integration of teams irrespective of geographical location, language barriers, and time zone differences. Embracing diversity in team composition not only enriches the development process with varied perspectives but also aligns with the global nature of modern business. This theme emphasizes the importance of adopting agile processes that are inclusive and considerate of these variances, ensuring that teams can collaborate effectively despite physical and cultural distances. Such an approach enhances communication, fosters a sense of unity, and leverages the unique strengths brought by diverse team members, thereby driving innovation and efficiency.

The final theme focuses on the critical need for a unified, transparent system that effectively communicates progress to all stakeholders. It's essential that this system not only caters to the internal dynamics of the development teams but also extends to external stakeholders, including customers, investors, and partners. This involves the use of standardized, accessible tools and processes that provide real-time updates and insights into the development process, ensuring that all parties are well-informed and aligned with the project's progress and objectives. Such a system is pivotal in maintaining stakeholder trust, facilitating informed decision-making, and promoting a culture of transparency and accountability.

In summary, the Adopting Agile Processes section lays out a comprehensive framework for agile outsourcing, emphasizing the need for innovative team management models, the incorporation of diverse and distributed teams, and the establishment of effective communication channels for stakeholders. These themes collectively forge a path towards a more resilient, adaptive, and inclusive approach to software development, aligning with the dynamic needs of modern businesses and the global nature of technology advancement.

F - Fully Integrated Team Ownership

The concept of Fully Integrated Team Ownership marks a pivotal phase in the journey of agile outsourcing. Once a company has established the ability to deliver products internally, cultivated a responsive and agile culture, and implemented processes that effectively operate across geographical and cultural boundaries, it's time to entrust the teams with greater autonomy and responsibility.

In this phase, the focus of management and executive leadership shifts to strategic oversight and talent acquisition, stepping away from the intricacies of day-to-day operations. This transition does not imply a withdrawal from being informed or involved but signifies a trust in the capabilities of the integrated teams, comprising both employees and outsourced talent. These teams, now equipped with the necessary tools, knowledge, and processes, are empowered to navigate the operational aspects of software development and product management.

This shift to team ownership encourages a self-sustaining and self-improving environment. Teams are not only responsible for the execution of tasks but also for identifying areas of improvement, innovating solutions, and implementing changes to enhance efficiency and output quality. This self-healing mechanism is fundamental to a mature agile outsourcing model, where continuous improvement is ingrained in the team's ethos.

Moreover, entrusting teams with ownership fosters a deeper sense of commitment and accountability. When teams know they are trusted and their decisions hold weight, it cultivates a more engaged and proactive workforce. This empowerment leads to higher motivation and satisfaction levels among team members, which in turn can lead to better retention rates and a stronger overall performance.

However, the transition to Fully Integrated Team Ownership requires careful management. Ensuring that teams are well-equipped with clear guidelines, access to necessary resources, and open channels for communication with management is crucial. Regular check-ins and strategic alignment sessions can help maintain a balance between autonomy and alignment with the company's broader goals.

In summary, Fully Integrated Team Ownership is not about relinquishing control but about evolving the role of leadership to enable teams to thrive independently. It's about building an environment where teams are confident and capable enough to drive the day-to-day operations, innovate, and self-improve, while leadership focuses on strategic growth and nurturing the company's vision and values. This approach not only leverages the full potential of an agile, distributed workforce but also paves the way for sustainable growth and innovation in an ever-evolving technological landscape.

Empowerment

Embracing Fully Integrated Team Ownership within an organization fundamentally revolves around the empowerment of various roles, ensuring they possess the autonomy and authority to effectively manage their respective domains. This empowerment is a cornerstone of a mature agile outsourcing model, where decision-making and accountability are distributed across the organization.

For Product Management, this empowerment translates into true ownership of the product, complete with profit and loss (P&L) responsibilities. Product managers must have the authority to make strategic and operational decisions about the product, based on their understanding of market needs, customer feedback, and financial implications. This level of autonomy enables them to act swiftly and decisively, without being hindered by the need for constant approvals from higher management. This empowerment, however, is balanced with accountability, ensuring that product managers are responsible for the outcomes of their decisions and the overall success of the product.

Similarly, fully integrated employee-outsourced development teams are entrusted with the day-to-day responsibilities of building and shipping software. These teams are equipped with the necessary tools, processes, and authority to manage their workflows, tackle challenges, and implement solutions independently. Empowerment in this context means that these teams are trusted to make technical and operational decisions, with management and executive leadership refraining from micromanaging or overriding established processes. Instead, leadership's role pivots to providing strategic guidance, resources, and support to enable these teams to perform at their best.

However, empowerment does not imply a lack of oversight or accountability. On the contrary, it means setting high standards and expectations for all roles within the organization. While teams are given the freedom to operate independently, they are also held accountable for meeting the objectives and quality standards set by the management. This accountability is crucial in maintaining alignment with the organization's goals and ensuring that the autonomy granted to teams leads to positive outcomes.

In essence, the shift to Fully Integrated Team Ownership and the accompanying empowerment of roles represent a significant cultural change within an organization. It requires a shift in mindset from both leadership and team members, fostering an environment where trust, responsibility, and accountability are integral to the operational fabric. By empowering product managers and development teams, organizations can foster a more dynamic, responsive, and efficient approach to software development and product management, driving innovation and success in a competitive technological landscape.

Resolution Management

In the intricate tapestry of software development, particularly in environments where teams are large and culturally diverse, the management of resolutions becomes a critical component for maintaining harmony and productivity. The expansion of teams, inclusive of both in-house employees and outsourced resources, inherently increases the probability of interpersonal conflicts. Mitigating these conflicts necessitates a proactive approach, fostering an environment that encourages open communication, respect, and understanding of cultural nuances.

When conflicts do escalate to a point where management intervention becomes necessary, it's imperative to adopt an impartial stance. Decisions shouldn't be swayed by the employment status of the involved parties; rather, they should be rooted in fairness and the overarching objective of delivering customer-centric products within a sustainable and healthy agile culture. Often, the root cause of these conflicts is miscommunication, which can be further complicated by cultural differences, particularly between more conservative and liberal cultures. Addressing these conflicts requires a respectful approach that acknowledges these cultural disparities while focusing on shared professional goals.

Facilitated communication is often key to resolving misunderstandings and differences. Creating channels and opportunities for open dialogue, where team members can express their perspectives and concerns, helps in fostering mutual understanding. However, it's crucial to recognize that not all conflicts are mere miscommunications. In instances where actual HR violations are involved, especially concerning outsourced resources, it's essential to involve vendor management.

Regular check-ins and a robust working relationship with vendor management are vital. These partners are typically keen to resolve any issues swiftly, but it's important to respect and defer to their HR policies and procedures. Nonetheless, in situations where the working environment becomes toxic, it's crucial to remember that you have the agency to request the removal of specific resources from your project. This action, though severe, may sometimes be necessary to preserve the integrity of the team and the quality of the work environment.

Ultimately, resolution management in a diverse, multi-sourced team environment requires a balance of empathy, cultural sensitivity, and a firm commitment to the principles of a healthy agile culture. By maintaining these values, conflicts can be addressed constructively, leading to stronger, more cohesive teams aligned with the common goal of developing exceptional software.

Fully Integrated Team Ownership Summary

Fully Integrated Team Ownership marks a transformative stage in agile outsourcing, signifying a company's readiness to entrust greater autonomy to its teams. This phase follows a successful establishment of internal product delivery capabilities, the cultivation of a responsive and agile culture, and the implementation of processes that transcend geographical and cultural barriers. It signals a shift in the role of management and executive leadership towards strategic oversight and talent acquisition, rather than day-to-day operational management.

In this phase, teams composed of both employees and outsourced talent are empowered to oversee the operational aspects of software development and product management. This empowerment fosters an environment where teams are responsible not just for task execution but also for identifying improvement areas, innovating, and applying changes to enhance efficiency and output quality. The model encourages a self-sustaining and continuously improving ethos, integral to a mature agile outsourcing framework.

The shift to team ownership enriches commitment and accountability. When teams understand their decisions and actions have significant impact, engagement and proactive participation are naturally enhanced, leading to higher motivation and job satisfaction. This, in turn, translates into better retention rates and overall performance.

However, transitioning to Fully Integrated Team Ownership requires deliberate management. Teams should have clear guidelines, adequate resources, and open communication channels with management to maintain a balance between autonomy and alignment with broader company goals.

This chapter emphasizes empowerment across various organizational roles. Product Management, for instance, is vested with true P&L responsibilities, allowing them to make strategic decisions without constant oversight. Similarly, integrated development teams are entrusted with the autonomy to manage their workflows and make significant operational decisions, supported by leadership that provides strategic direction rather than micromanagement.

Resolution management in this diverse and multi-sourced environment is crucial. Conflicts, often stemming from miscommunication and cultural differences, need to be addressed with fairness and a focus on shared professional goals. Vendor management plays a vital role, especially in conflicts involving outsourced resources, where their HR policies and procedures must be respected.

In conclusion, Fully Integrated Team Ownership is about evolving leadership roles to enable independent team operation, where trust, responsibility, and accountability are central. It's a shift towards a model where teams are fully capable of driving day-to-day operations, innovation, and self-improvement, while leadership focuses on strategic growth and nurturing the organization's vision and values. This approach maximizes the potential of an agile, distributed workforce and sets the stage for sustainable growth and innovation in the dynamic field of technology.

T - Tireless Continuous Improvement

The introduction to the "Tireless Continuous Improvement" section of our book marks a pivotal moment in the journey of agile software development and outsourcing. Having navigated through the complexities of establishing successful software development teams, fostering a healthy culture, and empowering teams to meet customer needs, your organization stands at a commendable juncture. The achievements up to this point are significant and worthy of recognition. However, it's crucial to understand that the level of excellence achieved should not be viewed as a final goal but as a baseline for further growth and development.

This part of the book delves into the philosophy of continuous improvement, a concept that transcends beyond mere procedural activities to become a fundamental mindset ingrained within the organization. Continuous improvement is about nurturing an environment where both leadership and team members are perpetually open to advancements in technological strategies, process optimizations, and the generation of innovative ideas. It's about creating a dynamic workspace where the pursuit of excellence is ongoing, and where the objective is not just to maintain the status quo of quality and efficiency but to elevate it consistently.

In this context, continuous improvement becomes an integral part of your organization's DNA. It means always striving to deliver more value to your customers, seeking ways to enhance quality, increase speed, and align more closely with customer demands and expectations. This relentless pursuit of improvement is what differentiates good organizations from truly great ones. It is what ensures that your teams are not just responding to the current needs of your customers but are proactively anticipating future requirements and adapting to meet them.

As we explore the concept of Tireless Continuous Improvement, we will delve into strategies and methodologies that can help instill this mindset within your teams. We will look at practical ways to encourage innovation, facilitate effective feedback loops, leverage new technologies, and refine processes for greater efficiency. The goal is to equip your organization with the tools and philosophies necessary to not just succeed in the present but to continue evolving and excelling in the ever-changing landscape of software development and customer expectations.

In essence, this section of the book is about embracing change as a constant and seeing continuous improvement not as an occasional initiative but as an ongoing commitment. It's about empowering your teams to always aim higher, push boundaries, and relentlessly pursue excellence in every aspect of their work.

Defining Continuous Improvement

Defining continuous improvement within the context of agile software development and outsourcing is pivotal to understanding how it reshapes traditional models of software creation and deployment. At its core, continuous improvement in software development is a paradigm that emphasizes persistent, incremental change. This approach aligns seamlessly with the principles of agile development, which advocates for adaptability, flexibility, and iterative progress.

In the realm of software outsourcing, continuous improvement presents a unique set of challenges and opportunities. It requires teams and their leaders to adopt a mindset geared towards constant evolution and enhancement of their processes and outputs. This mindset is crucial for navigating the complexities and uncertainties inherent in software development, particularly when teams are geographically dispersed or culturally diverse.

The essence of continuous improvement lies in its incremental nature. The changes implemented may vary in scale, from minor tweaks to significant overhauls, but their common goal is to drive better outcomes. These improvements are not one-time events but part of an ongoing cycle, continually refining and elevating the software development process. The magnitude of these changes is less important than the commitment to consistently seeking and implementing ways to enhance efficiency, quality, and alignment with project objectives.

Setting clear guidelines for these changes is essential. These guidelines should ensure that all improvements are aligned with the broader business objectives and strategies of the organizations involved. This alignment ensures that the efforts invested in continuous improvement translate into tangible benefits for the product and, ultimately, the business.

Ideas for continuous improvement in software development can originate from any level within an organization. They may stem from frontline developers, project managers, client feedback, or strategic insights from leadership. This openness to ideas from diverse sources is a hallmark of a healthy continuous improvement culture. It acknowledges that valuable insights can come from various perspectives and that everyone in the process has a role to play in driving improvement.

In summary, continuous improvement in software development and outsourcing is a dynamic and inclusive process. It is characterized by a commitment to ongoing, incremental change, a focus on aligning improvements with business goals, and an openness to ideas from across the organizational spectrum. This approach not only enhances the effectiveness of the software development process but also ensures that it remains responsive and relevant in a rapidly evolving technological landscape.

Importance of Continuous Improvement

The concept of continuous improvement in the realm of custom software development is fundamentally about enhancing existing processes rather than adding new layers of complexity. This approach underscores the idea that improvement is not about overhauling systems that are already functioning well but about refining and optimizing them. In various business sectors, continuous improvement is recognized for its potential to identify and enhance areas that could operate more effectively or efficiently. It's crucial for team leaders to understand that this is not an additional task for their software development team but a mindset that should permeate their approach to development.

As famously articulated by Steve Jobs, continuous improvement presents an opportunity to scrutinize and question existing practices in a more analytical and scientific manner. This mindset is especially relevant in the context of security testing and analysis within the Software Development Life Cycle (SDLC). By prioritizing continuous improvement, teams can identify and address problems, vulnerabilities, and errors early in the development process. Addressing issues in the initial stages is often simpler and more cost-effective than dealing with them post-deployment.

The importance of continuous improvement extends particularly to software security, a critical aspect of secure development programming. By understanding and addressing risks early in the SDLC—before any code is written or designs are implemented—teams can prevent many potential problems. This proactive approach is not only more cost-effective but also minimizes the likelihood of significant issues arising later, which can be more challenging and expensive to resolve.

Integrating the concept of continuous improvement throughout the SDLC involves several key practices:

1. Emphasizing Analysis: Regularly review and analyze what is being implemented to ensure it aligns with the project objectives and is being executed effectively.

2. Anticipating Risks: Continuously ask what could go wrong at each stage of development. Identifying potential risks early allows for timely mitigation strategies.

3. Simplifying Problem Resolution: Focus on creating systems and processes that make identifying and solving problems easier and more efficient.

4. Solution Definition and Execution: Clearly define solutions to identified problems and find feasible ways to implement these solutions within the existing development framework.

5. Iterative Review: Continuously go back and review the steps in the software development process. This iterative approach ensures that every phase of the development is refined and optimized for better outcomes.

In summary, continuous improvement in software development is about cultivating a mindset of ongoing refinement and optimization. It's about being proactive in identifying potential issues, emphasizing security, and ensuring that every stage of the development process is as efficient and effective as possible. This approach not only enhances the quality of the software produced but also contributes to a more agile, responsive, and robust development process.

Benefits of Continuous Improvement

Continuous improvement is a vital component in the journey of integrated outsourced and employee software development teams. Its significance becomes increasingly apparent when considering the scale and complexity of modern businesses. Here's an exploration of how continuous improvement profoundly benefits these blended teams:

At the heart of continuous improvement is the enhancement of product quality. By constantly refining processes, teams can identify and rectify defects early, leading to a more robust and reliable end product. This ongoing focus on quality results in software that not only meets but often exceeds customer expectations.

Continuous improvement drives teams to streamline their workflows, eliminate redundancies, and adopt more efficient practices. This leads to a more productive work environment where teams can accomplish more in less time, without compromising on quality.

By identifying inefficiencies and potential issues early in the development process, teams can avoid costly fixes and overruns later on. This proactive approach to problem-solving means less time and resources are spent on reworking or correcting errors, thus reducing overall development costs.

In line with lean principles, continuous improvement helps in identifying and eliminating waste - be it in resources, time, or effort. This not only optimizes resource utilization but also contributes to a more sustainable development practice.

When teams are empowered to improve their processes and see the tangible results of their efforts, it leads to greater job satisfaction. Furthermore, the collaborative nature of continuous improvement fosters stronger team bonds and a sense of shared achievement.

A workplace that values continuous improvement and personal development is more likely to retain its talent. Employees and contractors feel valued and part of a progressive, forward-thinking team, reducing turnover and the associated costs of recruiting and training new staff.

As product quality improves and delivery times shorten, customer satisfaction naturally increases. Happy customers are more likely to be loyal, repeat customers. By consistently meeting and exceeding customer expectations, you solidify your company's reputation as a reliable and customer-centric organization.

The underpinning philosophy of continuous improvement is that it's not just a set of actions but a mindset that permeates every aspect of the software development process. Teams that are encouraged to take ownership of their processes and outcomes are more likely to embrace this mindset, leading to a culture where improvement is a constant, integrated part of the work. This culture not only benefits the immediate software development teams but also has a ripple effect across the entire organization, contributing to its overall growth and success in a competitive business landscape.

Principles of Continuous Improvement

The principles of continuous improvement in the context of software development are centered around making small, incremental, and sustainable changes that collectively contribute to significant improvements over time. These principles are not just operational tactics; they represent a mindset that encourages constant evolution and refinement of processes and practices. Here are the core principles:

The essence of continuous improvement lies in making small and incremental changes. These are easier to implement and manage compared to large-scale overhauls. In software development, this could mean refining a code review process, optimizing a deployment pipeline, or enhancing a feature based on user feedback. These small adjustments, accumulated over time, lead to substantial improvements.

Empowering software developers to identify and address challenges is crucial. When developers are actively involved in spotting inefficiencies or bottlenecks in the development process, they become agents of change. This engagement not only improves the process but also boosts morale and fosters a culture of ownership and accountability.

Small, incremental changes typically require less investment compared to major shifts. For software engineers working in custom software development, this principle means continuously looking for ways to streamline processes or eliminate unnecessary steps, which can lead to cost and time savings.

: When team members are involved in the change process, they are more likely to see the value in these changes and are more inclined to embrace them. This sense of ownership is crucial for sustainable continuous improvement, as it encourages developers to be proactive in refining their work processes.

Continuous improvement is not a one-time event; it's an ongoing process. In the bustling world of software development, it's essential to maintain visibility and collaboration among team members. Utilizing automation tools and data solutions can aid in keeping all stakeholders informed about ongoing changes and their impacts in real-time.

To ensure that continuous improvements are effective, they need to be measurable. Tools and technologies, particularly in automation and data analytics, enable teams to track the effectiveness of the changes they implement. This measurability allows for a systematic approach to improvement, ensuring that changes are not just made for the sake of change but are genuinely enhancing the development process.

Implementing these principles requires a strategic approach, where leadership encourages a culture of continuous learning and improvement. By fostering an environment where small changes are celebrated, employee input is valued, and improvements are systematically measured and refined, software development teams can evolve their practices to become more efficient, productive, and aligned with the ever-changing demands of the industry.

Retrospectives

Of all the ceremonies involved in software development it's important to call special attention to sprint retrospectives because they play a pivotal role in the agile process, serving as a crucial mechanism for continuous improvement and team development. Held at the end of each sprint, these retrospectives provide a dedicated time for the team to reflect on the recent sprint's successes and challenges. This introspective approach is vital in fostering a culture of open communication and collaborative problem-solving. It encourages team members to share their experiences, insights, and suggestions in a constructive environment, enabling the identification of areas for improvement. Through retrospectives, teams can analyze what worked well and what didn't, allowing them to adjust their strategies, processes, and behaviors for future sprints. This iterative process of reflection and adaptation is essential for enhancing productivity, maintaining high team morale, and ultimately, delivering higher-quality software more efficiently. In an outsourced setting, retrospectives also bridge cultural and geographical divides, creating a shared understanding and aligning the team towards common goals, despite the distributed nature of their work.

Continuous improvement is not only a ceremony, it is also a mindset. Leadership and the teams should be encouraged to be continuously open to improved technological strategies, improved processes, and innovative product ideas.

Root Cause Analysis

Root cause analysis (RCA) is a critical process in software development, particularly when dealing with major issues, especially those that occur in a production environment. It's a systematic approach used to identify the underlying causes of faults or problems. The primary objective of RCA is not to assign blame but to understand what happened, why it happened, and what can be done to prevent its recurrence. This process is vital in creating a learning culture within both in-house and outsourced software development teams.

When a significant issue arises, it's important to convene a group of relevant individuals from various departments such as development, operations, product management, and support. These cross-functional teams bring diverse perspectives and insights, which are essential for a comprehensive analysis.

The RCA process begins with establishing a clear and detailed understanding of the issue, including the sequence of events leading to the problem and any immediate actions taken in response. This initial step is crucial for setting the stage for a deeper investigation.

A core technique used in RCA is the "5 Whys" method. This involves asking "Why?" in response to the initial explanation of the problem, and then continuing to ask "Why?" for each subsequent answer. After about five iterations of asking "Why?", the team usually reaches the underlying root cause of the issue. This iterative questioning helps peel back the layers of symptoms to uncover the fundamental problem.

Involvement of all relevant parties, including outsourced personnel, is essential in these discussions. Their expertise and knowledge can often be crucial in identifying the root cause. It's important to remember that these sessions are learning opportunities and should be approached with a mindset of growth and improvement, rather than punishment or blame.

Once the root cause is identified, the team collaborates to develop recommendations and action plans to prevent future occurrences. These might involve changes in processes, additional training, system modifications, or other preventive measures.

Sharing the findings from the RCA with the entire team is crucial. This transparency ensures that everyone learns from the incident and understands the changes implemented to prevent its recurrence. Encouraging questions and discussion around the RCA findings fosters a culture of continuous learning and collective responsibility.

The key to effective RCA is maintaining an environment where team members feel safe to openly discuss issues without fear of retribution. This openness not only leads to more effective problem-solving but also builds trust and strengthens team dynamics, crucial elements in the agile software development landscape.

What Happens When Teams Regress

When a strong continuous improvement culture occasionally leads to a dip in productivity or a decline in code quality, it's crucial to understand and address the underlying causes effectively. While metrics like velocity, cycle time, and escaped defects can signal such regressions, understanding their context is key to formulating appropriate responses. Here are some considerations for addressing different scenarios that might lead to these issues:

If a team's dip in performance is due to experimenting with new methods or technologies, it's important to maintain a supportive environment. Experimentation is a vital part of continuous improvement, even when it doesn't yield the desired results. These scenarios should be viewed as learning opportunities, and the team's willingness to innovate and take risks should be applauded. Encourage the team to analyze the experiment – what worked, what didn't, and how they can apply these learnings in future endeavors.

When team performance is affected by the absence of key members, such as due to vacations or unexpected leaves, it's important to assess the situation carefully. Discuss with the team whether bringing in temporary members would be more beneficial or disruptive. This decision should be made collectively, considering the team's dynamics and the specific challenges they're facing. In some cases, adjusting deadlines or re-prioritizing work might be a better approach than introducing new temporary team members.

Sometimes, teams may experience a slump without a clear external cause. This situation requires a sensitive and understanding approach. Engage with the team to identify potential root causes – these could range from burnout to unclear goals, or even interpersonal issues. Setting SMART goals can help the team refocus and regain their momentum. These goals should be realistic, clearly defined, and aligned with both the team's capabilities and the organization's broader objectives. It's essential to maintain a positive and encouraging atmosphere, emphasizing recent successes and realigning the team with their long-term objectives.

In cultures where pride and saving face are important, it's crucial to approach these discussions with sensitivity. Focus on collective goals and improvements rather than individual shortcomings. Emphasize that setbacks are a natural part of any innovative and dynamic work environment and that the team's overall growth and learning are what truly matter.

Ultimately, fostering a culture that values continuous improvement involves embracing both successes and setbacks as integral parts of the journey. By maintaining open communication, encouraging experimentation, and supporting teams through challenges, organizations can ensure that their continuous improvement efforts lead to sustainable growth and development.

Management Continuous Improvement

The commitment to continuous improvement should not be limited to development teams alone; it is equally crucial for management to embody this principle. As leaders, it is unreasonable to expect teams to strive for constant growth and enhancement if the same is not reflected in the management's practices. This commitment to self-improvement by management can have a profound impact on the entire organization, fostering a culture of growth, learning, and mutual respect.

The journey towards improvement for management begins with actively seeking feedback. This can be achieved through regular conversations, scheduled feedback sessions, introspective practices, or anonymous surveys. Such feedback mechanisms provide valuable insights into the team's perceptions, concerns, and suggestions for improvement. They serve as a mirror reflecting the effectiveness of management strategies and areas that require attention.

Upon receiving feedback, it is essential for management to critically evaluate it and implement small, incremental changes. These changes can be considered as experiments, with their effectiveness measured against key metrics such as team retention, developer satisfaction, project success rates, and overall team morale. It's important to note that not all changes will yield positive results, and that's perfectly acceptable. The key is to learn from these experiments, adapt, and continue evolving.

Transparency in management's continuous improvement journey is vital. When management openly shares their efforts to improve, it not only demonstrates accountability but also reinforces the culture of growth within the organization. Sharing the progress, the challenges faced, and the lessons learned helps in building trust and encourages a more open and collaborative work environment.

In cases where management decisions lead to unfavorable outcomes, it is crucial to conduct a thorough analysis to understand the root cause. Sharing the findings from this analysis, along with a clear action plan to address the issues, can be a powerful demonstration of accountability and commitment to improvement. This transparency not only helps in regaining the team's confidence but also serves as a learning opportunity for the entire organization.

In conclusion, continuous improvement in management is not just a responsibility; it's an opportunity to lead by example, demonstrating to the teams that growth and learning are integral to the organization's ethos. By actively engaging in their own improvement journey, managers can inspire their teams, foster a positive work culture, and contribute significantly to the overall success and resilience of the organization.

Tireless Continuous Improvement Summary

The "Tireless Continuous Improvement" section of your book is a comprehensive exploration of the importance of ongoing development and refinement in agile software development and outsourcing. It emphasizes the concept of continuous improvement as a core philosophy, not just a set of actions, advocating for a mindset that is always open to advancements and innovations. This section discusses strategies to nurture this mindset, such as encouraging innovation, facilitating feedback, and leveraging new technologies. It also highlights the need for management to exemplify continuous improvement, demonstrating commitment and transparency in their growth.

The section further explores the benefits of continuous improvement for integrated teams, including enhanced product quality, efficiency, and customer satisfaction. It stresses the importance of small, incremental changes, employee involvement, and the measurable impact of these improvements. Additionally, the role of retrospectives and root cause analysis in fostering a learning culture is detailed. Overall, the section conveys the message that continuous improvement is key to maintaining a competitive edge and achieving sustainable success in the dynamic field of software development.

S - Synchronized Work

At this stage in our journey, we've successfully built a robust software production system, combining skilled product management, development, release, operations, and support. This system, powered by a mix of in-house and outsourced staff, already places us ahead of many competitors. However, for those aiming to push the boundaries even further, this section introduces the concept of Synchronized Work. It's about transforming our operations into a 24/7, globally responsive unit, utilizing a synchronized development framework. This approach leverages different time zones, enabling multiple teams across the world to collaboratively and continuously tackle projects, much like a round-the-clock factory but with global knowledge workers.

Principles of Synchronized Work

In the realm of synchronized work, a multi-faceted approach ensures seamless collaboration and efficient progress across diverse teams. Central to this approach is the ability of product management to adeptly break down larger projects into smaller, manageable units of work. This decomposition is not just about dividing tasks but ensuring that each segmented feature reaches a 'ready for release' state. Such precision allows for customer-ready features to be integrated smoothly into the continuous deployment release train or scheduled frequent releases, ensuring a steady flow of new functionalities to users.

Underpinning this system is a robust continuous integration framework. This vital component acts as the backbone of the development process, ensuring that various components of a broader feature synergize effectively. It plays a crucial role in maintaining the integrity of the collective work, preventing individual developers' changes from inadvertently disrupting the whole. This system is a safeguard against potential conflicts or errors that could arise from concurrent development activities.

Consistency in user experience is another cornerstone of synchronized work. Establishing design and interface standards is key to achieving this uniformity. These standards ensure that despite the segmented development process, the end product presents a cohesive and seamless user interface, enhancing the overall experience for the end-users.

Effective communication and knowledge transfer are facilitated through daily handoffs. These handoffs are pivotal in maintaining continuity, as they ensure that as one team concludes their day, the incoming team is fully apprised of the progress and current state of work. This systematic exchange of information is critical in maintaining momentum and avoiding knowledge gaps that could impede progress.

The orchestration of work shifts is done with a keen eye on promoting a healthy work-life balance for each team member. Aligning shifts to accommodate the various time zones and personal needs of team members is not just about efficiency; it's about ensuring that each individual is working at their optimal level. This balance is vital for fostering an environment where creativity, engagement, and innovation can thrive. In this way, synchronized work is not merely a methodological approach to software development but a holistic strategy that considers the well-being and potential of every team member, thereby enhancing the overall quality and output of the work.

Synchronized Work vs Follow the Sun

The synchronized work method proposed in this book significantly differs from the well-known "Follow the Sun" (FTS) model, popularized by companies like IBM and General Electric. In FTS, the focus is on continuous work on a monolithic product, with teams around the globe handing off ownership at the end of their shifts. This requires extensive management oversight and coordination through synchronization meetings, leading to a heavier managerial overhead.

Conversely, the synchronized method emphasizes the integration of smaller components rather than managing a single, large product. This approach relies on standardized processes and tooling rather than on management overhead, aiming to reduce errors and increase the development velocity. It avoids the daily "getting up to speed" phase common in FTS, as each team works more independently on distinct components of the project. However, this method demands more skillful coordination from product management to ensure that the final integrated product meets all requirements and maintains consistency. This approach is generally less prone to errors and can result in a higher velocity of product development due to reduced overhead in handoffs and daily orientation.

Synchronized Workflows

In the synchronized workflow approach outlined in your book, the process of software development is strategically streamlined for efficiency and effectiveness. It starts with product management identifying high-priority features during backlog grooming sessions. These features are then broken down into smaller, manageable stories, ideally designed to be completed within 1-2 days. This decomposition, aided by input from technical teams, ensures that components are prioritized and bundled to increase the likelihood of completing essential elements within a single development cycle. While sequencing work, it's important to clearly label dependent work so that the same team can pull it in or special arrangements can be made to coordinate cross-teams, but this should be avoided if possible.

Development kicks off with the use of feature flags, enabling product management to control the activation of features upon completion. This stage is crucial as teams develop components following their standard procedures, integrating their work into a heavily automated Continuous Integration/Continuous Deployment (CI/CD) pipeline. This automation is key in ensuring that all components work harmoniously together.

Throughout the development phase, the product team actively tests these components in lower-tier environments, checking for seamless integration and overall functionality. Finally, once the code is fully deployed in the production environment and all components are verified to fit well, the product team activates the feature for customers by flipping the feature flag. This systematic approach not only streamlines the development process but also ensures a high degree of product quality and customer satisfaction.

If all goes well, large features can be released to production in a fraction of the time of sequential workflows. Let's say you're working on a feature that would take a normal team 2.5 sprints to complete. If you're on a 2 week sprint schedule, this is up to 6 weeks before a feature is available in production. Under the Synchronized system proposed here, it would be possible for 3 teams to release the feature in only 1 sprint, or 2 weeks. Substantially decreasing the time to customer value.

Cross-Team Context

In the realm of synchronized work patterns, where features are collaboratively developed by multiple teams, the sharing of context is not just helpful but essential. Each team must understand the why, who, and what of the features they are contributing to. The 'why' pertains to the purpose behind the feature: what problem it aims to solve or what value it intends to add. The 'who' focuses on the target audience, ensuring that the teams are aware of the end-users' needs, preferences, and behaviors.

Equally important is the 'what' — the concrete details of the feature's requirements. This includes clear guidelines on UI and UX patterns, which are critical for maintaining consistency in the user experience. Teams need a firm grasp on the expected user interactions with the feature, as this knowledge shapes the development approach and influences design choices.

Moreover, there is a need for a comprehensive understanding of how each component, developed by different teams, will fit together into a unified whole. This understanding is crucial for ensuring that all pieces of the puzzle align correctly to form a feature that delivers on its promise of customer value. Sharing this detailed context across all teams involved in the feature's development fosters a unified vision. This shared vision ensures that all teams are aligned in their objectives, working efficiently and effectively towards a common goal, leading to a product that resonates with users and fulfills its intended purpose.

Unqualified Work

In the framework of synchronized work, it's vital to discern which tasks are suitable for this methodology. Primarily, tasks that are small in scale, such as a quick bug fix or a modest enhancement that can be effectively completed by a small team in a short timeframe (typically 1-2 days), do not fit well into the synchronized work pattern. This is primarily because the intricacies and coordination efforts required for synchronized work do not align with the simplicity and straightforwardness of these tasks. The value of synchronized work lies in its ability to efficiently manage larger, more complex projects where multiple teams' input and collaboration significantly enhance the development process. For smaller tasks, the overhead of distributing detailed information across several teams and managing their collaboration can be counterproductive, overshadowing the simplicity and quick turnaround of such tasks. Therefore, while the principles of systematic automation and robust CI/CD processes are universally applicable, their implementation in the context of small-scale tasks should be judiciously considered to maintain efficiency and effectiveness.

Handling Miss Synchronizations

In the dynamic world of software development, even the most mature and capable teams occasionally encounter unexpected complexities in their projects. When a unit of work turns out to be more intricate than initially estimated, it can disrupt the flow of the project, especially in synchronized work environments where multiple teams are collaborating. In such scenarios, it's crucial to have a flexible and responsive approach to project management.

The first step in addressing these unforeseen challenges is to reassess and reevaluate the work that has been done. This might involve returning to the grooming and decomposition stages, where the project is broken down again into smaller, more manageable units. Product management plays a key role in this phase, analyzing the progress and re-prioritizing the tasks based on the new insights and time estimates provided by the development teams.

One possible outcome of this reassessment is adjusting the feature rollout plan. This might mean releasing a version of the feature that is less complete than originally intended, allowing for incremental improvements in subsequent updates. Alternatively, product management may decide that it's more prudent to delay the entire feature release, ensuring that when it does launch, it meets the full scope and quality expectations.

The critical aspect of this process is maintaining open lines of communication between all stakeholders. Development teams need to provide clear and realistic updates on their progress and challenges, while product management must be adept at quickly assimilating this information and making informed decisions about the project's direction. This agility in decision-making is a hallmark of a mature agile environment, where adapting to new developments is part of the standard operating procedure.

Finally, it's important to remember that adjusting plans based on new developments is not a sign of failure, but rather a demonstration of a pragmatic and adaptive approach to software development. By embracing flexibility and maintaining a focus on delivering final customer value, teams can navigate through unexpected complexities and still achieve successful project outcomes.

Synchronized Work Summary

In concluding the "Synchronized Work" part of our book, we reflect on the journey to creating a 24/7 globally responsive software production system. This part highlights the shift to Synchronized Work, a model that utilizes time zones to keep product development continuous, akin to a round-the-clock factory but with global knowledge workers. We've explored the principles of breaking down projects into smaller tasks, ensuring each feature is ready for release, maintaining a strong continuous integration system, setting design and interface standards, implementing effective daily handoffs, and aligning work shifts for a balanced work-life dynamic. We've differentiated this approach from the traditional "Follow the Sun" model, emphasizing less management overhead and more efficient, error-free production. The synchronized workflow stresses the importance of feature flags, continuous testing, and CI/CD automation. We also acknowledged that smaller tasks may not fit this model and advised on handling unexpected complexities and the importance of flexibility in project management. This section underscores the transformative potential of Synchronized Work in achieving faster, more efficient, and collaborative software development.

Communication Bringing It All Together

By now you should have a firm idea on how to successfully integrate outsourced software developers into your product development process. Now let's discuss some binding glue to bring it all together.

Communication, undoubtedly, serves as the vital glue binding together every element of the CRAFTS methodology in Agile Outsourcing. This section aims to emphasize the pivotal role of effective communication in ensuring the success of an Agile Outsourcing strategy.

At the core of Agile Outsourcing, communication transcends mere exchanges of information; it embodies the spirit of collaboration, understanding, and mutual respect. Effective communication is the linchpin that aligns Code Delivery Capability with business objectives, ensuring that what is developed truly aligns with customer needs. It fosters a Responsive Agile Culture by enabling swift adaptation to changes and challenges. In adopting Agile Processes, communication is the channel through which teams navigate complexities and synchronize their efforts, ensuring that processes are not just adopted in theory but practiced effectively.

The concept of Fully Integrated Team Ownership hinges on transparent and open communication. It allows for a seamless fusion of in-house and outsourced teams, nurturing a sense of collective responsibility and shared purpose. This is where communication strategies must be robust and tailored to overcome geographical, cultural, and linguistic barriers. Tireless Continuous Improvement is fueled by feedback loops, retrospectives, and honest dialogue about successes and areas for growth. Synchronized Work is only possible through consistent and clear communication, ensuring that all teams, regardless of their location, are aligned and moving in the same direction.

In this section, we delve into how organizations can cultivate an environment where communication is not an afterthought but a core strategic component. It involves exploring tools, practices, and cultural shifts necessary to facilitate effective communication. This includes leveraging technology for better collaboration, fostering an organizational culture that values and encourages open communication, and developing strategies to navigate and embrace cultural diversity within global teams.

Ultimately, this section underscores that while the CRAFTS methodology provides a robust framework for Agile Outsourcing, its success is largely contingent upon the quality, consistency, and effectiveness of communication within and across teams. It's about creating a dialogue that is not just about transmitting instructions but about building relationships, understanding context, and working together towards a common vision. The goal is to transform communication from a routine task into a strategic asset that drives the success of Agile Outsourcing initiatives.

Risk

In modern software development, the complexity and scale of projects often lead to underestimation of the required work. This is where embracing risk as a primary communication tool becomes pivotal. Risk, in this context, is not a negative element but a crucial aspect of project management. Communicating risks effectively helps in identifying potential delays, design flaws, or external factors that may impact project success.

Teams should be encouraged to openly discuss risks related to schedules, product functionality, and external influences. This open communication of risks enables the entire team to engage in proactive problem-solving and mitigation strategies. It is essential for teams, especially those from diverse cultural backgrounds where discussing problems might be frowned upon, to understand the importance of transparent communication. Emphasizing that risk communication is valued and rewarded, and not a cause for reprimand, is key to changing this mindset.

In some cases, there might be a misconception that discussing risks is a way of making excuses. However, in a culture where teams are fully empowered, communicating risks is seen as a responsible action and a request for support, rather than an excuse for non-performance. Empowered teams, which take pride in their work, use risk communication as a tool to maintain high standards and seek assistance when needed.

This approach to risk communication fosters a more collaborative, open, and effective project environment, where potential issues are addressed promptly, reducing the likelihood of surprises that can derail large projects. By prioritizing risk communication, management can ensure that projects stay on track, adapt to challenges efficiently, and ultimately lead to successful outcomes.

Relationships Cross Boundaries

In the context of globally distributed software development teams, the importance of fostering real human interactions and relationships cannot be overstated. These connections go beyond mere professional collaboration. Team members, often separated by vast geographical distances, might have only superficial or stereotypical understandings of each other's cultures, potentially influenced by media portrayals. It's essential to break through these barriers by encouraging teams to learn about each other's backgrounds, interests, and lifestyles.

Creating opportunities for team members to connect on a personal level, sharing stories, experiences, and cultural nuances, helps build a foundation of mutual respect and understanding. This personal connection is particularly vital in a remote working environment where physical interactions are limited. Encouraging curiosity and empathy towards each other's lives fosters a work culture where individuals are seen and valued not just as 'coding robots,' but as whole people with diverse perspectives and experiences. This human-centric approach to team building is crucial for developing strong, collaborative relationships that underpin effective communication and successful project outcomes.

Face to Face

In the world of outsourced software development, face-to-face communication takes on a unique significance, distinct from collocated teams. It's crucial to facilitate in-person interactions, though they may be infrequent due to geographical distances. Prioritizing meetings between outsourced leadership (like architects and team leads) and product management is key. These core groups form the backbone of daily operations, and personal bonds forged through face-to-face meetings can significantly enhance the efficacy of self-organized teams.

In the absence of regular in-person contact, the next best approach is to ensure consistent visual communication during virtual meetings. Keeping cameras on during daily scrums and other ceremonies can maintain and strengthen interpersonal bonds. Visual cues can be invaluable, especially when language barriers exist. Being able to see each other helps in recognizing confusion or misunderstanding, allowing for timely clarification and empathetic responses. This practice is not just about maintaining professional rapport; it's about nurturing a deeper understanding and connection among team members, which is vital for the success of globally distributed teams.

Simple and Direct

Effective communication with outsourced teams, especially in a global context, necessitates the use of simple and direct language. This approach is instrumental in overcoming language and familiarity barriers, ensuring that all team members, regardless of their native language or cultural background, can understand and contribute effectively. To achieve this, it's advisable to avoid using slang, colloquialisms, or industry-specific jargon that might not be universally understood. Instead, opt for short, well-structured sentences and clear, straightforward language. A useful guideline is to communicate in a manner that would be comprehensible to a 6th grader, ensuring clarity and accessibility. This method of communication not only facilitates better understanding but also fosters an inclusive environment where every team member feels valued and able to participate fully.

The practice of confirming understanding is crucial in communications, particularly in settings involving outsourced teams where language and cultural differences might lead to misunderstandings. It's essential, after conveying information, to ask team members to paraphrase or repeat back their understanding of what was discussed. This ensures that the message was received as intended and clarifies any ambiguities. This method of verification should be reciprocal; you should also restate your understanding of what others communicate to you. This approach not only aids in clear communication but also helps break down hierarchical barriers that might prevent team members from expressing confusion or seeking clarification. Over time, as mutual understanding and communication patterns solidify, this practice may become less necessary. However, in the early stages of team collaboration, it's a vital tool for building effective communication channels and ensuring that all team members are on the same page.

Write It Down

The importance of documenting important messages in writing is a crucial aspect of effective communication, especially in a setting that involves diverse teams, possibly spread across various geographies and time zones. When a message is important, ensuring it is captured in a written form, be it via chat, presentation, a project management tool, or email, is vital. This practice serves multiple purposes:

1. Reference: Written records provide a reference point that can be revisited by team members for clarification or recollection of

details. This is especially helpful in complex projects where multiple discussions and decisions occur over time.

2. Clarity: Writing down messages helps to minimize ambiguity. It offers an opportunity to structure thoughts and present information in a clear, concise manner. This is particularly beneficial when dealing with teams that have varying levels of proficiency in the primary language used for communication.

3. Avoiding Misinterpretation: Written communication can reduce the risk of misinterpretation or loss of critical details that might occur in verbal exchanges. It provides a concrete record of what was discussed, agreed upon, or instructed.

4. Accountability: Documenting messages in writing fosters accountability. Team members can refer back to written communications to ensure they are adhering to the agreed-upon tasks, deadlines, or strategies.

5. Inclusivity: Writing down messages ensures that team members who were not present in a live conversation, possibly due to time zone differences, are not left out. They can catch up on discussions and contribute their input at their convenience.

In video chats or virtual meetings, it's a good practice to summarize the key points in writing during or immediately after the conversation. This reinforcement aids in ensuring that all participants have a common understanding of the discussion's outcomes. These written summaries can be shared with all relevant parties, ensuring that everyone, regardless of their participation in the actual meeting, is informed.

In conclusion, writing down important messages plays a critical role in ensuring effective communication, especially in a global team setting. It helps in maintaining clarity, preventing misunderstandings, ensuring accountability, and promoting inclusivity.

Establish Communities

In a diverse and globally distributed software development environment, the formation of communities plays a pivotal role in fostering collaboration, setting standards, and facilitating learning. These communities, centered around common interests or expertise areas, are self-organized groups where members from different teams come together to share knowledge, discuss challenges, and develop cross-team standards.

1. Formation and Purpose: Communities are typically formed around key aspects of software development, such as Architecture, User Experience, or Automated Testing. They provide a platform for individuals with similar roles or interests to connect, exchange ideas, and work towards common goals. The purpose of these communities goes beyond mere discussion; they aim to drive innovation, standardize practices across teams, and enhance the overall quality of work.

2. Communication Channels: For these communities to function effectively, having dedicated communication channels is crucial. Tools like Slack channels, forums, or even regular virtual meetings provide a space for ongoing dialogue. These channels serve as a hub for sharing updates, asking questions, or coordinating collaborative efforts.

3. Regular Meetings and Activities: Communities should meet regularly to discuss ongoing projects, new technologies, and emerging trends in their field. These meetings can take various forms, including workshops, presentations, or informal catch-ups. The key is to maintain a regular cadence of interaction that keeps the community engaged and informed.

4. Cross-Team Collaboration: One of the significant benefits of these communities is the facilitation of cross-team collaboration. By bringing together members from different teams, communities help in breaking down silos and encouraging a more integrated approach to problem-solving. This collaboration is particularly beneficial in large organizations where teams might be working on interrelated projects but lack a common platform for interaction.

5. Continuous Learning and Improvement: Communities are an excellent vehicle for continuous learning. They provide members with opportunities to learn from each other's experiences, explore new methodologies, and stay updated on industry best practices. This collective learning contributes to the professional growth of individuals and the evolution of the team as a whole.

6. Empowerment and Ownership: By being self-organized, these communities empower members to take ownership of their areas of expertise. They encourage proactive involvement in shaping practices and standards, fostering a sense of responsibility and pride in their contributions.

In conclusion, communities within a software development setting are more than just groups with shared interests. They are dynamic ecosystems that contribute significantly to the advancement of skills, the standardization of practices, and the fostering of a collaborative culture. By embracing the concept of communities, organizations can leverage the collective knowledge and expertise of their teams, driving innovation and excellence in their software development endeavors.

Country Specific Tips

Working effectively with outsourced software development teams from different countries requires understanding and adapting to their unique cultural and communication styles. Here are some tips for collaborating with professionals from India, the Philippines, Mexico, Poland, and China:

Argentina: Argentine professionals often exhibit a blend of formality and warmth in their business interactions. Personal relationships are important, so take the time to engage in small talk and get to know your colleagues on a personal level. Argentines are expressive and may communicate with emotion, but they also value respectful and polite dialogue. Decision-making can be hierarchical, so understanding the structure of the team and directing queries or discussions appropriately is important.

Brazil: Brazilians are known for their friendly and warm communication style. Building personal relationships and trust is crucial in Brazilian business culture. Informal and personable communication is often preferred, but it's important to maintain professionalism. Brazilians may communicate in a more indirect and high-context manner, so be attentive to non-verbal cues. Patience is key, as decision-making can sometimes be slower, given the emphasis on building consensus and relationships.

China: Working with Chinese professionals requires an understanding of the importance they place on hierarchy and respect. Communication tends to be indirect, and preserving 'face' or dignity is crucial. Avoid direct confrontation or criticism in public settings. Building a relationship, known as 'Guanxi,' is vital in Chinese business culture. This involves developing mutual trust and understanding over time. Decision-making can be hierarchical, so be patient with the process. Additionally, understanding basic Mandarin phrases or using a translator can be beneficial in showing respect and willingness to engage with their culture.

Costa Rica: Professionals in Costa Rica are known for their friendly and approachable demeanor. Business communication is often informal yet respectful. Building personal relationships is important, and taking the time to engage in small talk can strengthen your working relationship. Costa Ricans are generally punctual and value clear, direct communication, but they may avoid confrontation. Be sensitive to their communication style, ensuring clarity without being overly aggressive or blunt.

Czechia (Czech Republic): When communicating with Czech professionals, it's important to be straightforward and factual. Czechs generally appreciate directness and clarity in business discussions. They tend to be pragmatic and value efficiency, so keep your communications concise and to the point. Establishing initial formalities is important, but once a relationship is built, they often become more informal and open. Punctuality is highly valued in the Czech business culture, so make sure to be on time for meetings and adhere to deadlines.

Egypt: In Egypt, business culture places a high value on personal relationships, so it's beneficial to invest time in relationship-building. Egyptians tend to be warm and personable in their business interactions. While English is commonly used in business settings, incorporating some basic Arabic phrases can be well-received. Egyptians appreciate respect for their culture and traditions. Meetings may start later than scheduled, so patience is important. Communication can be indirect, so pay attention to non-verbal cues.

Estonia: Estonian professionals are known for their directness, efficiency, and high level of digital literacy. Communication is typically straightforward and to the point, with less emphasis on small talk. Estonians value punctuality and clarity, so be concise and precise in your communications. They appreciate a straightforward approach to problem-solving and decision-making. While Estonians may initially appear reserved, they are generally open and cooperative once a relationship is established.

India: Communication with Indian professionals often reflects a blend of indirectness and politeness. It's important to be clear and explicit in your instructions to avoid misunderstandings. Indians often use non-verbal cues, so pay attention to their tone and hesitations, which can indicate uncertainty or disagreement. Building personal relationships is valued, so take the time to engage in small talk before diving into business discussions. Be aware that Indians might avoid saying 'no' directly to maintain harmony and respect. Encourage open dialogue and create an environment where they feel comfortable sharing honest feedback.

Mexico: Mexican professionals typically appreciate a warm, personable approach to communication. Establishing a friendly relationship and showing interest in their culture can go a long way in building trust.

Mexicans often communicate in a polite and indirect manner, so it's crucial to read between the lines and understand the context. They also value group consensus, so involve the team in decision-making processes when possible. Face-to-face meetings or video calls are preferred over written communication, as they help in establishing stronger personal connections.

Nigeria: Nigerian professionals are known for their strong communication skills and openness to new ideas. English is widely spoken, facilitating easy communication. In Nigeria, respect for hierarchy and seniority is important, so be mindful of this in your interactions. Nigerians are generally direct in their communication but appreciate politeness and respect. Building personal relationships and trust is important, so invest time in getting to know your Nigerian colleagues beyond just business matters.

Philippines: Filipino professionals are known for their friendly and accommodating nature. They often communicate in a non-confrontational manner, so be sensitive to their reluctance to express disagreement directly. Establishing a rapport and showing respect for their opinions can encourage more open communication. Filipinos value 'pakikisama,' which means maintaining smooth interpersonal relationships. Understanding this cultural aspect can help in building a cohesive and collaborative working environment. Regular and clear communication is key, and providing specific feedback can guide them effectively.

Poland: Communication with Polish professionals is usually direct and to the point. They appreciate clarity and straightforwardness in business interactions. However, it's important to balance directness with politeness and respect. Poles value their time, so ensure that meetings are well-organized and efficient. They also respect hierarchy, so be clear about roles and responsibilities within the team. Building professional relationships based on mutual respect and trust is essential for effective collaboration with Polish teams.

Romania: Romanian professionals typically value clear and open communication. They are often willing to engage in detailed discussions to understand project requirements fully. It's important to show respect for their opinions and expertise. Romanians appreciate when their international partners make an effort to understand their culture. While English is commonly spoken in business settings, including some basic Romanian phrases in your communication can be seen as a sign of respect and effort to connect.

South Africa: South Africa's diverse culture reflects in its business practices. Communication tends to be straightforward and to the point. Punctuality and professionalism are important, and while initial meetings may be formal, relationships often become more relaxed over time. South Africans value clear, concise communication and appreciate when others respect their time. It's also important to be aware of and sensitive to the cultural and linguistic diversity within the country.

Ukraine: Ukrainian business culture values direct and open communication. While initial interactions may be formal, Ukrainians often develop more personal relationships over time. Respect for hierarchy is noticeable, so it's important to acknowledge and engage with senior team members appropriately. Ukrainians are generally punctual and expect the same from their partners. English is increasingly used in business settings, but being aware of and showing respect for the Ukrainian language and culture can enhance mutual understanding.

Vietnam: In Vietnam, business communication tends to be formal and respectful. Establishing relationships and trust is important for effective collaboration. Vietnamese professionals may be more reserved and less direct in their communication, so it's important to be patient and understanding. Showing respect for seniority and hierarchy is crucial in Vietnamese culture. Decision-making can be collective and consensus-driven, so involve the team in discussions and respect their input. Being aware of cultural nuances and showing respect for Vietnamese customs and traditions can greatly enhance working relationships.

In summary, successful communication with outsourced teams requires cultural sensitivity, patience, and adaptability. Understanding the nuances of each culture can enhance collaboration and lead to more productive working relationships.

Sensitivities

Finally, navigating cultural sensitivities is a crucial aspect of global team management, especially in a diverse workforce involving outsourced teams. Understanding and respecting cultural differences is key to creating an inclusive and harmonious work environment. This involves being mindful of topics that could be considered sensitive or taboo in different cultures, such as religion, politics, and alcohol consumption.

An example that illustrates the importance of this sensitivity is the use of the term "America." In some contexts, referring to the United States as simply "America" can be perceived as exclusive or offensive, particularly by individuals from South America who also identify as Americans. This highlights the importance of being aware of how certain terms or references might be received by international colleagues.

When informed about such sensitivities, it's crucial to adapt communication styles accordingly. If a team member points out a potential cultural misstep, it should be seen as an opportunity to learn and grow, not as a criticism. This learning and adapting process is a part of building strong, respectful relationships with team members from different backgrounds.

The goal is to ensure that all team members, regardless of their location or cultural background, feel respected and safe. Avoiding potentially sensitive topics is not about restricting conversation but about fostering a work culture that is considerate and inclusive. By focusing on common professional goals and interests, teams can build strong bonds and work effectively together while respecting each other's cultural norms and values.

Diversity Within a Diverse Workforce

Embracing diversity within outsourced teams is a crucial step towards fostering innovation and enhancing productivity in software development. Diverse teams bring a wealth of perspectives and ideas, often leading to more creative solutions and robust products. In my own experience, teams led by women engineers have proven to be exceptionally productive and reliable.

However, promoting diversity goes beyond just including different nationalities or cultures. It involves creating an inclusive environment for all minority groups within the regions you operate in. This includes ensuring opportunities for neurodivergent individuals, and understanding and addressing biases related to ethnic groups, tribes, castes, religious affiliations, and even regional or city versus village backgrounds.

Collaboration with the leadership of your outsourced firms is key to aligning their practices with your organization's values on diversity and inclusion. It's essential to communicate the importance of embracing diversity not just as a policy, but as a fundamental aspect of your company culture. By expanding the recruitment pool to include a diverse range of talents and backgrounds, you open up avenues for discovering some of the most innovative ideas and exceptional engineering talents. This approach not only enriches the work environment but also contributes significantly to the success and competitiveness of your organization.

IT Infrastructure

In the realm of synchronized software development, ensuring that outsourced teams have seamless access to IT infrastructure is crucial for efficient workflow. This involves extending key resources such as project management tools, source code control systems, CI/CD pipelines, cloud management interfaces, and various environments, including production, under controlled circumstances. The infrastructure can be extended using two main strategies:

Utilizing platforms like GitHub, Azure DevOps, or AWS DevOps offers easy and accessible solutions. These cloud-based tools enable access from virtually anywhere while maintaining high-security standards. Implementing best practices in security configuration, identity and access management (IAM), and aligning with Chief Information Security Officer (CISO) directives are essential steps in this approach.

For teams that require access to internally hosted tools, coordination with the internal IT team is necessary. Options include setting up a site-to-site VPN for teams located in a singular geographic location. It's important to conduct thorough audits of the local network configurations to ensure secure and exclusive access. Additionally, individual VPN services can be arranged for scenarios where team members work remotely. Compliance with internal controls and regulatory standards is a critical aspect of this setup.

In both scenarios, it's paramount to maintain stringent security measures and ensure that the setup facilitates the needs of the outsourced teams while adhering to the organization's security and compliance policies.

Holidays

Navigating holidays in the context of globally dispersed outsourcing teams presents unique challenges but also opportunities for cultural exchange and learning. With every country, and sometimes every region within a country, observing different national and local holidays, planning becomes a complex task. To mitigate potential disruptions, maintaining a comprehensive, publicly accessible holiday calendar is essential. This calendar should be a key reference point for product management and all teams, facilitating better planning and coordination of roadmaps and sprints.

Beyond mere scheduling, recognizing and celebrating these diverse holidays can be a meaningful way to engage with the cultural backgrounds of your team members. It's an opportunity to show respect and appreciation for the traditions and customs that are important to them. Acknowledging these holidays, even when their significance might not be fully understood by you or the team, strengthens team bonds and enhances mutual respect. By embracing these differences, you not only navigate the logistical aspects of holidays but also enrich the team's collective experience and understanding.

When it comes to vacation norms, there is a significant variance across different countries and cultures, each with its own customary practices and legal mandates regarding time off. Understanding and respecting these differences is crucial for maintaining a harmonious and productive working relationship with outsourced teams.

For instance, European countries are known for their generous vacation policies, often offering several weeks of paid leave as a standard. This is a stark contrast to the United States, where vacation days are typically fewer. Similarly, countries like Brazil and Australia also have a more liberal approach to vacation time. In Asia, the perspective on vacation varies widely, with some cultures emphasizing the importance of long working hours and others gradually adopting more liberal leave policies.

As a manager working with globally distributed teams, it's essential to be supportive of these differing approaches to vacation. It is not just about complying with legal requirements but also about acknowledging and valuing the cultural importance of rest and recreation in these regions. Employees who feel their cultural norms are respected are more likely to be satisfied and loyal to the company.

Planning for these variances in vacation time is similar to how one might plan for holidays—through proactive and strategic scheduling. It involves keeping a comprehensive calendar that accounts for the vacation times of all team members, regardless of their location. This calendar should be made available to everyone involved, facilitating cross-team awareness and planning.

It's also important to communicate with outsourced teams well in advance to understand their vacation plans. This allows for better project management, where deadlines and deliverables can be adjusted to accommodate the absences. Encouraging teams to cross-train and share knowledge can also mitigate the impact of team members being away on vacation.

Encouraging and respecting vacation time doesn't just benefit individual employees; it can also have a positive impact on the team and the company as a whole. Well-rested employees often return to work re-energized, with a renewed sense of creativity and motivation, which can lead to increased productivity and innovation.

In conclusion, recognizing and planning for the different vacation cultures across countries is an essential aspect of managing outsourced teams. Being supportive and accommodating of your team's vacation needs not only respects their right to time off but also builds a culture of trust and respect, which is the foundation of any successful global team.

Integrating Cybersecurity Into Your Process

First, it's important to note that outsourced software development can be secure, but in order to make sure of this, you must take certain precautions and steps to make sure it is intentionally secure. It's best to ensure you hold them to the highest standards and integrate them into your common security controls. Finally, this isn't a point in time activity, it's an ongoing activity, year after year.

Assessing Your Risk

In the contemporary landscape of software development, cybersecurity has ascended as a non-negotiable facet of managing outsourced teams. The initial step in embedding cybersecurity into your outsourced projects is a comprehensive risk assessment. This crucial measure illuminates potential vulnerabilities, allowing for proactive risk mitigation strategies to be established.

A robust risk assessment begins with a meticulous inventory of applications that are or will be in development by the outsourcing partner. Each application must be evaluated to discern its unique risk profile, including potential operational disruptions and adverse impacts on critical business functions such as shipping and order processing. The implications of these risks extend beyond operational hiccups, often carrying significant financial repercussions. By quantifying the business impact in monetary terms, organizations can prioritize resources effectively, focusing on areas where risk mitigation is most critical.

Equally imperative is the scrutiny of the security and infrastructure landscape that underpins the entire software development lifecycle, from conceptual design to final deployment in a production environment. In the case of methodologies that demand high levels of collaboration like Agile, it's essential to adopt a holistic viewpoint of all digital interactions between your enterprise and the outsourcing entity. This encompasses a thorough evaluation of how design documents, code repositories, and deployment strategies are managed and safeguarded.

The risk assessment should not merely be a one-time activity but rather an ongoing process that adapts to the evolving nature of threats and the project's progression. An experienced cybersecurity firm can bring to the table a nuanced understanding of potential risks and the expertise to develop a risk management plan that aligns with both the technical and business objectives of the outsourcing partnership.

By taking a comprehensive approach to risk assessment, organizations can establish a secure foundation for their outsourced development projects. This strategic foresight not only protects the company's assets but also fortifies trust with the outsourcing partner, ensuring that both parties are aligned in their commitment to security and quality throughout the product's development.

Train Your Outsourced Teams

In the realm of software development outsourcing, equipping your external teams with proper training is as pivotal as training your internal teams. This comprehensive approach ensures that your outsourced teams are not only technically proficient but also aligned with your company's cybersecurity and compliance standards.

First and foremost, conducting OWASP Top 10 training for your SaaS development teams is crucial. This training, ideally delivered by a reputable provider, will familiarize the outsourced team with the most common security risks associated with web applications. Understanding these vulnerabilities is key to preventing security breaches and maintaining the integrity of your software.

Secondly, teaching outsourced teams how to conduct security code reviews is an essential skill. These reviews are a vital part of the development process, enabling the early detection and remediation of potential security vulnerabilities in the code. By training outsourced teams in this area, you ensure that the code they produce meets your security standards before it progresses to further stages of development.

Another critical aspect is making sure that the outsourced teams are well-versed in your company's cybersecurity and compliance policies. They should have a clear understanding of these policies and the practical steps required to adhere to them. This knowledge is fundamental in ensuring that the work they do aligns with your organizational standards and regulatory requirements.

Lastly, integrating your outsourced team into your Static Application Security Testing (SAST) and Dynamic Application Security Testing (DAST) processes is imperative. Your external team should be proficient in using these systems, which play a significant role in identifying potential vulnerabilities within the application code and during its runtime. They must be trained on how to interpret the results from these tools and take appropriate corrective actions.

By investing in this comprehensive training regimen, you not only elevate the capabilities of your outsourced teams but also fortify the overall security posture of your software development process. It's a strategic move that pays dividends in terms of both product quality and compliance, ensuring that your outsourced software development aligns with the high standards you set for your internal teams.

Secure Coding Guidelines

Penetration Test

Regular penetration testing of your outsourced partner is a critical component of maintaining robust cybersecurity. This process involves a systematic attempt to breach the defenses of your systems and applications, similar to how an attacker might. Here's how to effectively implement this strategy:

1. Hiring a Reputable Firm: Choose a respected and experienced cybersecurity firm to conduct your penetration tests. A reputable firm will have the necessary expertise and tools to thoroughly assess the security of your systems and identify potential vulnerabilities. Ensure that they have a proven track record and relevant certifications in the field of cybersecurity.

2. Frequency of Testing: Conduct penetration testing regularly, ideally every six months. Continuous penetration testing services are also available from some providers, offering ongoing monitoring and testing of your systems. Regular testing helps to identify and address new vulnerabilities as they emerge and ensures continuous improvement of your security posture.

3. Collaboration with the Partner: Inform your outsourcing partner about the planned penetration tests. This collaboration is crucial for defining the scope of the test and ensuring that all legal and contractual boundaries are respected. Surprising your partner with an unscheduled test can lead to legal issues and damage the trust in your partnership.

4. Vulnerability Scanning: Complement penetration tests with regular vulnerability scanning. While penetration testing is an active attempt to exploit vulnerabilities in a system, vulnerability scanning is a more passive approach that identifies potential vulnerabilities without exploiting them. Scans can be automated and performed more frequently, offering a broader view of your cybersecurity status.

5. Service Level Agreements (SLAs) for Remediation: Your contract with the outsourcing vendor should include SLAs that specify the timeframe within which identified vulnerabilities must be remediated. This ensures that any security gaps are promptly addressed, minimizing the risk exposure.

By implementing these steps, you can ensure a comprehensive approach to testing the security of your outsourced projects. Regular penetration testing and vulnerability scanning provide an in-depth evaluation of your cybersecurity defenses, revealing areas that need strengthening. By working closely with your partner and a reputable testing firm, you can maintain high security standards, protecting both your interests and those of your customers.

DevSecOps

DevSecOps is an approach that integrates security practices within the DevOps process. It bridges the traditional gap between IT and security while ensuring fast and safe delivery of code. In the realm of DevSecOps, security is a shared responsibility integrated from the start of the development cycle. This integration reduces vulnerabilities and brings security closer to IT and business objectives.

Integrating DevSecOps into a process that includes outsourced software development teams requires a multifaceted strategy. Firstly, it's crucial to establish a culture of security within both in-house and outsourced teams. This involves training and awareness programs to ensure every team member understands their role in maintaining security. Communication plays a vital role here, as clear and continuous communication channels between in-house and outsourced teams ensure everyone is on the same page regarding security protocols and practices.

Secondly, incorporating automated security tools is essential. These tools can scan for vulnerabilities, ensure compliance, and automate certain security checks. They should be integrated into the Continuous Integration/Continuous Deployment (CI/CD) pipeline. This automation enables early detection of vulnerabilities and ensures that security is a part of the daily workflow without adding excessive overhead.

Thirdly, implementing strong governance and compliance standards is necessary. When working with outsourced teams, it's important to define clear security policies and procedures. This may involve regular security audits, adherence to standard security frameworks, and ensuring that outsourced partners have strong security practices in place.

Furthermore, embracing a shift-left approach, where security is considered from the very beginning of the software development life cycle, is also crucial. This proactive approach ensures that security is not an afterthought but a fundamental aspect of the development process.

Finally, continuous monitoring and feedback loops should be established. Regular monitoring of code, infrastructure, and applications for security issues is essential. Additionally, fostering an environment where feedback is actively sought and acted upon can lead to continuous improvement in security practices.

In summary, integrating DevSecOps into your process with outsourced software development teams involves fostering a culture of security, utilizing automated security tools, enforcing strong governance, embracing a shift-left approach, and establishing continuous monitoring and feedback mechanisms. This holistic approach ensures that security is an integral and seamless part of the development process, aligning with both the speed of DevOps and the security needs of the organization.

Certifications

Encouraging your outsourced developers to obtain specific security certifications is a strategic move that can significantly enhance the security and integrity of your software development projects. These certifications not only equip developers with crucial skills but also demonstrate a commitment to maintaining high-security standards in software development. Here's a look at some key certifications and their relevance:

1. EC-Council Certified Secure Programmer (ECSP): This certification focuses on the fundamental aspects of secure programming. It is designed to equip developers with the

necessary skills to prevent security breaches and vulnerabilities from the outset of the programming process. ECSP certification ensures that developers are adept at writing code that is not only functional but secure against modern threats.

2. Certified Secure Software Lifecycle Professional (CSSLP): This certification is essential for developers involved in the software development lifecycle. It validates their ability to incorporate security practices in each phase of the software development process, from design to deployment and maintenance. CSSLP-certified professionals ensure that security is an integral part of the development process.

3. GIAC Secure Software Programmer-Java (GSSP-JAVA): For teams working with Java, this certification is vital. It demonstrates a deep understanding of Java security features and common pitfalls. GSSP-JAVA certified developers are proficient in writing secure code in Java, thereby safeguarding Java-based applications from prevalent security threats.

4. GIAC Certified Web Application Defender (GWEB): This certification is designed for developers specializing in web applications. It equips them with skills to build secure web applications, understand common web application security issues, and implement defense strategies against web-based attacks.

5. GIAC Secure Software Programmer – .NET (GSSP-.NET): This is a crucial certification for developers working with .NET framework. It validates their ability to write secure code in .NET and protect applications from vulnerabilities specific to .NET environments.

6. Certified Ethical Hacker (CEH): The CEH certification is for developers who wish to understand hacking tools and techniques from an ethical standpoint. This knowledge enables them to anticipate and counteract hacking attempts, thereby fortifying the security of their applications.

7. Certified Encryption Specialist (CES): This certification is essential for developers who work with encryption

technologies. It indicates proficiency in encryption principles, deployment, and management of encryption solutions. CES-certified developers can ensure data security through effective encryption strategies.

Encouraging your outsourced development teams to obtain these certifications not only enhances their skill set but also aligns their work with global security standards. This results in a more secure and robust software development process, reducing vulnerabilities and instilling greater confidence in the security of your software products. Additionally, certified developers can bring valuable insights and practices to your projects, contributing to a culture of security awareness and continuous improvement in your development practices.

Preparing for the Unexpected

In the realm of agile outsourcing, it's imperative to consider the impact of global events on your software delivery capabilities. The world is interconnected, and events in one part of the globe can have ripple effects that reach your outsourced teams. This section of our book doesn't delve into exhaustive strategies for every potential scenario, but it aims to highlight the importance of awareness and preparedness for global disruptions, which could include:

Economic conditions like currency fluctuations and inflation can have a profound impact on your outsourcing partnerships. For instance, countries like Turkey and Argentina have experienced significant inflation rates, which can affect the cost structures and financial stability of your outsourcing agreements. Keeping an eye on these trends helps in proactively adjusting your strategies and financial planning.

Natural calamities like earthquakes, floods, or hurricanes can disrupt the operations of outsourced teams. Understanding the geographical risks and having contingency plans in place is essential to mitigate the impact on your software delivery.

Political instability and conflicts, such as the war in Ukraine, can have direct and devastating impacts on your outsourcing operations. Ukraine, for example, is a hub for outsourced software development, and the conflict there poses significant risks to businesses relying on Ukrainian IT services.

To navigate these complexities, maintaining a strong and supportive relationship with your outsourcing partners is key. Open communication channels, understanding, and a supportive approach during tough times align with the principles of our book and foster a resilient and adaptable outsourcing partnership.

Additionally, staying informed about global events is crucial. Regularly reading comprehensive sources like The Economist can provide insights into global trends and events, helping you make informed decisions and prepare for potential disruptions. Awareness, combined with a strategy that prioritizes support and adaptability, can guide you through the uncertainties of global events, ensuring the sustainability of your software delivery.

Choosing The Right Outsourced Partner

When selecting an outsourced software development partner for staff augmentation, several critical factors must be taken into account to ensure that the partnership is successful and aligns with your organization's objectives and values.

The technical expertise and skills of the potential partner are paramount. It is essential that they possess proficiency in the technologies and programming languages pertinent to your product. Their team should not only match the skill level of your in-house team but ideally surpass it in some areas, offering a blend of expertise that enhances your existing capabilities. This synergy is vital for a seamless integration of outsourced and in-house resources, leading to a more robust and versatile development team.

The experience of the outsourcing partner in handling projects similar to yours cannot be overstated. A partner with a track record of industry-specific projects will likely understand your needs better and can hit the ground running. Their past projects serve as a testament to their ability to handle the nuances and complexities of your domain.

Effective communication is the backbone of any successful collaboration, especially in outsourcing scenarios. The ability of the partner's team to communicate effectively in your preferred language and their adherence to strong communication practices ensure that project nuances are not lost in translation and that collaborative efforts are productive.

Cultural fit is another critical aspect of the partnership. The partner should share your organization's values and work style. This alignment ensures that they can integrate into your processes and company culture smoothly, reducing friction and facilitating better teamwork.

An outsourced partner's project management capabilities should be compatible with your preferred methodologies. Whether you follow Agile, Scrum, or any other development methodology, the partner should be adept at these practices, ensuring that project management is coherent and unified across teams.

Scalability and flexibility of the partner are also significant. They should be able to adjust team sizes to accommodate project demands promptly. This might involve having a large pool of developers ready to be deployed or a robust recruiting process that can quickly bring in new talent as required.

The quality assurance processes of the partner must be rigorous and should align with your high standards. Robust testing and quality control measures are non-negotiable to ensure the product meets the desired quality benchmarks.

While cost is a consideration, it should be balanced against the quality and value offered. It is often advisable to avoid the lowest cost vendors, as they may not attract or retain the best talent, which is essential for high-quality software development.

Security and intellectual property protection measures are crucial. The partner must demonstrate the ability to implement and adhere to stringent security protocols to protect your data and intellectual property.

Client references and testimonials offer valuable insights into the reliability and performance of the partner. Feedback from companies similar to yours can provide assurance about the partner's ability to deliver as promised.

Lastly, thought leadership is an indicator of a partner's expertise and standing in the community. Those who contribute through technical meetups, blogs, and reports not only showcase their knowledge but also demonstrate their commitment to the broader technology community. Such partners are often at the forefront of their practice areas and can bring innovative ideas and practices to the table.

In conclusion, finding the right outsourced software development partner for staff augmentation requires a multi-dimensional evaluation, focusing on technical acumen, relevant experience, communication efficacy, cultural harmony, flexible project management, scalability, quality assurance, cost-effectiveness, security practices, positive client references, and thought leadership. A partner that excels in these areas is likely to be an asset to your software development efforts, driving your projects towards success.

Negotiating the Right Contract

Negotiating terms with an outsourced partner is a crucial step in establishing a successful collaboration, particularly under a staff augmentation contract. Here's an in-depth look at the key elements to consider during negotiations:

Scope of Work and Deliverables: Begin by meticulously defining the scope of work. Detail the tasks, responsibilities, and expected deliverables of the outsourced team. It's essential to align on the project goals, establish clear timelines, and set any critical milestones. A mutual understanding of the expected outcomes lays a strong foundation for the partnership.

Pricing and Payment Terms: The pricing model should be transparent and mutually agreed upon. While hourly rates offer flexibility, they can also introduce unpredictability in budgeting, hence, weigh the options carefully. Avoid milestone-based payments, which may constrain agile practices. Clarity on the frequency and method of payments will prevent future misunderstandings.

Resource Allocation and Team Composition: Clearly outline the specifics regarding the team's size and composition, ensuring the right mix of skills and experience. Include provisions for scaling the team according to project demands. Introduce approval clauses for senior-level resources to maintain quality control, especially in the initial stages of the engagement.

Intellectual Property Rights: Intellectual property rights are paramount. The contract should unequivocally state the ownership of any developments. Aligning IP protection with your company's tax strategy is also vital for long-term operational efficiency.

Confidentiality and Non-Disclosure: Robust confidentiality clauses and NDAs protect sensitive information. If the vendor services competitors, include terms to prevent any overlap of resources that might lead to conflicts of interest.

Compliance and Legal Jurisdiction: Address compliance with relevant industry standards and legal regulations, particularly when working across borders. Establish the governing legal jurisdiction for the contract, as this will dictate how legal disputes are managed.

Termination Clauses: A solid contract outlines the circumstances under which either party can terminate the agreement. This includes stipulated notice periods and procedures for an orderly wind-down or transition of work.

Dispute Resolution: Incorporate a fair and clear dispute resolution process to manage potential disagreements, which could range from mediation to arbitration.

Technology and Infrastructure: Discuss and agree upon the technology stack and infrastructure to be used, ensuring compatibility and seamless integration with your existing systems.

Training and Onboarding: If there is a need for the outsourced team to understand your internal processes, tools, or culture, negotiate the terms for training and onboarding.

Discount Tranches: Include clauses for price discounts based on the number of hired resources over time, and consider pre-negotiated discounts for longer-term engagements. Be mindful of potential annual price adjustments due to inflation.

Auditability: Ensure you have the right to perform compliance audits or that the vendor maintains necessary audit compliance standards.

Evaluation Criteria: Establish clear criteria for evaluating the success of the project, ensuring that these are measurable and agreed upon by both parties.

Bonuses: While direct bonuses for individual team members might be challenging, consider a bonus structure for the vendor to share in the success, fostering a partnership mentality.

Travel Expenses: Define who will bear the costs of travel, which is significant for ensuring face-to-face interactions, and under what conditions this will occur. This facilitates the planning of necessary in-person meetings that are crucial for relationship building and project success.

By thoroughly negotiating these aspects, you can establish a strong and clear agreement that will serve as the guiding framework for your collaboration with an outsourced software development partner.

Conclusion

Embarking on the journey of transforming outsourced software development into a formidable competitive edge is a venture that demands meticulous planning, steadfast dedication, and a deep understanding of both the technical and human facets of business. This book has served as a guide to achieving such a transformation, outlining an approach that pivots on empathy, trust, and a methodical application of the CRAFTS methodology.

The CRAFTS framework lays the foundation for success in outsourced software development. It begins with 'Code delivery capability', ensuring that the technical proficiency and processes are in place to deliver high-quality software consistently. 'Responsive Agile culture' follows, which is about cultivating an environment that rapidly adapts to changes and embraces the principles of Agile to stay ahead of the curve. 'Adopt Agile processes' further reinforces the need to implement and adhere to Agile methodologies that are scalable and flexible across geographic and cultural boundaries.

'Fully integrated Team Ownership' is the linchpin of the CRAFTS approach, emphasizing the empowerment of teams to take charge of their work, fostering a sense of accountability and pride in their contributions. 'Tireless Continuous Improvement' advocates for an organizational mindset where evolution and growth are constants, driving teams to relentlessly seek enhancements in every aspect of their work. Lastly, 'Synchronized work' encapsulates the strategic coordination of global teams working in harmony to maintain continuous development and delivery, optimizing the benefits of time zone differences.

By embracing the CRAFTS methodology, organizations can achieve rapid realization of customer value, staying several strides ahead of their competitors. This approach enables a pace of innovation that is swift and sustainable, ensuring that products not only meet market demands but also anticipate future needs. Moreover, it cultivates a profound understanding of customers, their environments, and their evolving requirements, allowing for solutions that are truly customer-centric.

The book has underscored the importance of empathy in managing outsourced relationships—seeing teams as partners rather than mere vendors. Trust is the currency of this realm, where mutual confidence between in-house and outsourced teams becomes the bedrock for successful collaboration. Through the diligent application of the CRAFTS methodology, organizations can navigate the complexities of outsourced software development with grace and efficiency, turning potential challenges into strategic advantages.

In conclusion, this book is not just about the technicalities of software development; it is a narrative of transformation. It is about how organizations can align their operations, culture, and strategies to not just participate in the global marketplace but to lead and redefine it. It is a testament to the power of human-centric approaches in the realm of technology and a call to action for leaders to innovate, integrate, and inspire teams across the world to achieve greatness together. The CRAFTS methodology is more than a framework; it is a pathway to reimagining what is possible when we harness the collective expertise, creativity, and passion of a globally distributed workforce.

ABOUT THE AUTHOR

About The Author Joseph Pearce Joseph Pearce is a seasoned expert in the realm of managing outsourced teams, bringing nearly two decades of rich experience to the table. His journey in the outsourcing industry is marked by extensive work in domestic outsourcing, nearshoring, and offshoring, showcasing a deep understanding of the global dynamics of team management. Joseph's expertise extends across continents, having built and led teams in North America, South America, Europe, and Asia. This diverse exposure has equipped him with a unique perspective on cross-cultural team dynamics and the intricacies of managing geographically dispersed teams.

Throughout his career, Joseph has been dedicated to honing and implementing effective software development practices that are not only robust but also scalable. His ability to manage large-scale projects, overseeing hundreds or even thousands of resources, stands as a testament to his exceptional leadership and strategic skills. His approach has always been forward-thinking, focusing on how to seamlessly integrate agile methodologies within the outsourcing framework.

In his book, Joseph Pearce delves into the wealth of knowledge and insights he has gathered over the years. He shares the lessons learned from the numerous experiments he conducted, all aimed at refining the process of outsourcing in an agile environment. The book is not just a reflection of his professional journey, but also a practical guide that encapsulates the essence of his tried and tested strategies. Readers will find themselves equipped with the knowledge to navigate the complexities of outsourced team management, all while maintaining efficiency and fostering innovation. Joseph's book is an invaluable resource for anyone looking to master the art of outsourcing in today's fast-paced and ever-evolving business landscape.

Printed in the USA
CPSIA information can be obtained
at www.ICGtesting.com
LVHW021325210324
775134LV00009B/38